IT'S A DONE DEAL

It's A Done Deal

The Miracle Babies of Grace Church

Joseph Carlucci Adevai
with Steven B. George

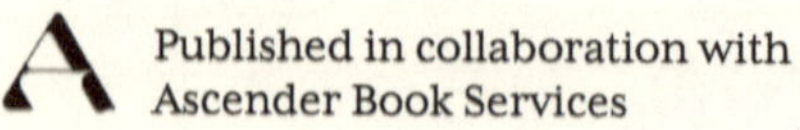

Published in collaboration with
Ascender Book Services

Table of Contents

Underlined chapters denote perspective-switching narratives.

For You formed my inward parts;

You knitted me together in my mother's womb.

I praise You, for I am fearfully and wonderfully made.

Wonderful are Your works;

my soul knows it very well.

My frame was not hidden from You,

when I was being made in secret,

intricately woven in the depths of the earth.

Your eyes saw my unformed substance;

in Your book were written, every one of them,

the days that were formed for me,

when as yet there was none of them.

PSALM 139:13–16 (ESV)

Coincidence or God-Incidence

Inception

WHEN I FIRST started Grace Church in the year 2000, I wasn't hoping to be dubbed "the baby pastor." If you traveled back in time and dropped that name on me then, chances are I wouldn't have known what to make of it. But if you stopped by in 2004, after I met Debbie Nannery, things might have been different.

Debbie was a powerful addition to our freshly formed worship team. In fact, I think she was probably our first real "worship leader." She and her husband were a powerhouse couple with a distinct heart for God, and I don't think it was a coincidence that the more they got involved with the church, the more we grew.

The Nannerys never brought it up themselves, but it eventually got back to me that they had spent years, unsuccessfully, trying to have a child. Yes, *years*. Most people know that just one year like that is long enough to be considered infertile. And you know what? That bothered me.

I wasn't sure why it hit me so hard, but I remember feeling almost angry. Angry that this family, a lifeline for my own as we struggled through our church's infancy, had to endure the repeated sting of negative tests. I was reminded of a story in the Gospel of Luke, where Jesus heals a woman crippled by an evil spirit that forced her to walk completely hunched over. He calls her a "daughter of Abraham." I thought to myself, *Isn't Debbie a daughter of God?*

One day, during our altar call—the end of service when congregants come forward for prayer—I called her down from the stage where she had been singing. Right there, I prayed for her and her husband, believing with everything in me that she would conceive. That faith was tested in the months that followed as their battle with infertility continued. Eventually they decided to give up on a natural conception and pursue adoption.

"Sure, if that's what you feel is right," I said when they approached me. "If you'd like, we'll even write you a letter of recommendation. But, honestly? My wife and I believe you're getting pregnant. So . . . keep trying?"

The same week that the adoption papers went through, the Nannerys came back to me with news that would forever change my life.

It was the first time a couple I had prayed for conceived after years of infertility. And though I didn't realize it then, it was the first domino in a long chain of events that would earn me the unofficial title of "the baby pastor."

The House of God

Looking back, I can see that Debbie's story was the start of something I never could've planned. I didn't set out to become known for praying over couples who couldn't conceive, but things started to trend that way. One story became two, two became ten. Before long, the nickname began to stick.

When I first prayed for the Nannerys, I became aware of the pain felt by those who were infertile. With a small battalion of six children by that point, I had plenty of my own problems, but having kids wasn't one of them. The more I thought about it, the more it stirred something in me. I had never before given it real thought, but it worked on my mind. This was a modern wound that God clearly cared about, and maybe through our humble little house, God was working to do something about it.

Back in 2004, we were a young congregation, full of faith, but still learning what it meant to be a spiritual family. I was still learning what it meant to be a pastor. It's been an educational twenty-plus years since then. I started out preaching to a congregation of ten or less, and am now seeing between two and twenty-five people a week come forward to give their lives to Christ. We can't take credit for that; it's all God. He has brought us such a long way: from a fledgling family to a full-blown house of grace.

Over the years, I've seen families walk into our sanctuary burdened by disappointment and walk out holding hope again. I've prayed with couples who had nearly given up and celebrated alongside them when the impossible became possible. These stories changed me as much as they did them.

Hope Infusions

This book is a collection of modern-day miracle stories. They are accounts of God still at work in the lives of people who dared to believe when everything else told them not to. It isn't theory or theology. It's testimony.

Somewhere along the way, we decided that faith and reason can't coexist. We've grown quick to label the extraordinary as coincidence or luck. Yet, I've watched too many "coincidences" unfold in front of me to believe that God has stopped working. Miracles may not look the same today as they did when Jesus walked the earth, but they do still happen, and the people in this book can testify to that.

I don't mean to sound naive or out of touch. I know that words like *faith* and *miracles* can sound hollow when life gets complicated. A lot of people might even say, "Of course you'd tell me to have faith; you're a pastor." But if I'm being honest, I'm not preaching faith *because* I'm a pastor. Rather, I'm a pastor only because of the results of faith. I committed my life to Christ because He met me at a time when I had none at all.

What I've witnessed in my own life is that faith is more than a sentimental idea. Where our faith meets despair, God shows Himself faithful. Keeping with that, consider this book a case study of faith and the greatest miracle of all: the miracle of life.

What This Book Isn't

Before we go any further, I need to make something clear. This book is not a formula for getting what you want from God or a parenthood manual. It's not a guarantee that everyone who prays will conceive.

Every story in these pages is unique. Some experienced a radical, full healing. Others met God in miracles of circumstance or learned to trust Him in ways they never had before. Each journey is sacred in its own way. I've prayed with families who saw miracles and others who are still waiting. Both kinds of prayers matter to God. Faith isn't only proven by results, but also our willingness to trust even when the outcomes don't match our expectations.

I don't claim to know why God works the way He does. I'm not special, and there's no power in my hands. But I've learned that when He moves, He does so out of love and purpose in ways we can't fully understand or predict. These stories aren't meant to glorify any one person. They're testimonies meant to glorify the God who still intervenes in human lives today.

The Word of Our Testimony

Talking about what God has done is equally (if not more) important than simply experiencing it. Why? Because our faith itself is built on testimony.

The Bible is divinely inspired, but it wasn't written by a magic finger on stone tablets from start to finish. It's mostly a collection of testimonies from ordinary people who, under the Holy Spirit's direction, carefully documented the miraculous events they had witnessed. Their testimonies became scripture itself. For example, this means that men like Matthew and John probably kept careful notes of Jesus's life and then polished them into final drafts. Under the guidance of the Holy Spirit, their testimonies became two of the Gospels.

In His final direct command to His closest disciples, Jesus asked them to be His "witnesses," spreading the good news of His death and resurrection. As their testimony advanced, so did the Christian faith. The early believers valued their testimony so deeply that many chose death over recanting.

Altogether, scripture is a compilation of forty authors, spanning three continents over fifteen hundred years. Yet it all works together to tell one story with Jesus at its center. In the book of Revelation, it says that believers will overcome by "the blood of the Lamb and the word of our testimony." That's not just poetry. It's a call to action. It is how we combat hopelessness in a world wrought with despair.

4 One generation shall commend Your works to another, and shall declare Your mighty acts.
PSALM 145:4 (ESV)

The faith of all believers is built on the testimonies of those who preceded us. In the same way, the faith of every couple in this book was built upon the testimonies of those who came before. And now, their stories have become their own testimonies that will echo forward into generations.

The Heart of God, the Theology of Life

The spiritual side to family life and childbirth is rooted in more than just superstition or human tradition. In fact, God's design for marriage and family can be traced right back to the very beginning when He created humanity and placed them in an earthly paradise. A paradise that we can hardly imagine now in our modern world of concrete jungles.

> *27 So God created man in His own image, in the image of God He created him; male and female He created them.*
> *28 And God blessed them. And God said to them, "Be fruitful and multiply and fill the earth and subdue it, and have dominion over the fish of the sea and over the birds of the heavens and over every living thing that moves on the earth."*
> **GENESIS 1:27–28 (ESV)**

There's a lot to dive into theologically here, but let's focus on the fact that "being fruitful" and "multiplying" landed at the very top of God's list. God valued our ability to procreate so much that he instituted sex within the bounds of marriage as something beautiful and blessed. Contrary to what you might've heard, Christians *do* value sex highly. The big difference in our view to the culture's view is that we also value sex as *holy*.

When God gave us the earth, He blessed us and basically said: "Now get to work, fill this place with little yous, and show them the wonders of everything I've made." In this, the act of having and raising children, can be found a beautiful picture that symbolically mirrors God's creation of us in His own image.

The ability to multiply is a gift from God. Each one of my children and the experiences I owe to them have given me a profound appreciation for life. Fatherhood feels like the culmination of everything I've ever worked for. Everything you've learned and conquered takes on new meaning when you have little ones that are depending on you. As parents, we respond to a divine call and are responsible for building hope in a better tomorrow.

The God Who Restores

Hope is a major theme of scripture. In the Gospels are recorded thirty-seven miracles of Jesus Christ during His time on Earth. It's the power of these stories that kept me from suicide in a moment when I didn't feel I had a reason to live. Taking even just five of those thirty-seven as examples, we see formative ideas about God, even just by looking at a surface level:

Water Turned to Wine—*Gospel: John*
Jesus saves a wedding celebration. God delights in celebration, marriage, and family.

The Bleeding Woman Healed—*Gospels: Matthew, Mark, Luke*
In Jesus's healing of a woman who had been bleeding menstrually for eight years, we see God reverse chronic pain and longtime suffering in response to relentless faith.

Jairus's Daughter Revived—*Gospels: Matthew, Mark, Luke*
Jairus's daughter dies of an illness while Jesus is on the way to heal her. Jairus and the people at his house believe there's nothing else to be done, but God renews hope even when it's "too late."

Lazarus Raised from the Dead—*Gospel: John*
Lazarus is raised even after he has been laid to rest in a tomb. God's timing is impeccable, even when nature brings finality.

The Centurion's Servant Healed—*Gospels: Matthew, Luke*
Jesus points out the unprecedented faith of a high-ranking pagan official who had no religious obligation to believe in Him. The power of humble, radical, childlike faith touches the heart of God.

These miracles reveal a God who values faith, restoring the broken, healing the sick, and turning shame or mourning into joy. This God is still at work today.

Let's Talk Numbers

And believe me, we absolutely *need* Him at work today. Listed below is some research on infertility, childbirth, and parenthood:

- 17.5% of the adult population experience infertility. This is roughly 1 in 6 worldwide.[1]
- In the US, 1 in 5 (19%) of women between the ages of 15 and 49 with no prior births can't get pregnant after a year of

1 1 in 6 People Globally Affected by Infertility: WHO," World Health Organization, April 4, 2023, accessed December 5, 2025, https://www.who.int/news/item/04-04-2023-1-in-6-people-globally-affected-by-infertility

trying. Around 1 in 4 (26%) have trouble getting pregnant or carrying a pregnancy to term.[2]

- The Mayo Clinic says that miscarriages end about 10–20% of known pregnancies, but the true number is likely higher.[3]

The simple fact is that it's getting harder and harder for couples today to conceive, and this is part of the fertility wound that I feel the church is primed to address. The Mayo Clinic wrote that, as of 2023, fertility rates are at an all-time historic low. That's definitely a blow to God's family design, but the data shows that it isn't a statistical majority of couples in this fight. Because of that, infertility is often something that gets wrestled with in silence. Pregnancy tests are read and discarded behind closed doors. If you're suffering with this, it can feel like it's only happening to you.

The church needs to be on the front lines of this family crisis because it's not going anywhere. We need to be counseling couples through their marriages, counseling young parents on the do's and don'ts of raising children. Those who are struggling to conceive need our prayers, belief, and support in their grief. God cares about this. We should too.

---

2   "Infertility: Frequently Asked Questions," Centers for Disease Control and Prevention, last modified May 15, 2024, https://www.cdc.gov/repro-ductive-health/infertility-faq/index.html.

3   "Miscarriage," Mayo Clinic, accessed December 5, 2025, https://www.mayoclinic.org/diseases-conditions/pregnancy-loss-miscarriage/symptoms-causes/syc-20354298.

God Is Not a Deadbeat Dad

Repeat after me: God is not a deadbeat dad. Have you repeated it out loud? Good. Keep that in your mind at all times. God is not a deadbeat dad, and that means that He's invested in being a part of your life. A good dad doesn't just put food on the table, but also makes time to inquire into his children's lives and interests. When you decide to live life with God, you're agreeing to live *every* part of your life with Him. He isn't a dad that's "too busy" for you. He's the kind of dad that comes home from a long day and asks you to play catch in the yard so he can ask you about your day.

7 casting all your anxieties on Him, because He cares for you.
  1 PETER 5:7 (ESV)

People tend to compartmentalize their lives into God-boxes and non-God-boxes. I'm telling you that doing life with God means letting Him into *all* the boxes. He cares about it all, and that especially includes deep desires like the wish to have kids.

Many people separate childbirth from God, even though he emphasized it from the moment our species became conscious. Anyone who's explored how life is created in the womb, how a young human develops and grows, will tell you that it's a miracle in and of itself. God's care for humanity extends from Eden to every delivery room today.

Diving In

As you turn these pages, you'll encounter the lives and struggles of families who learned what true faith really means. Each story is unique, shaped by joy and loss, prayer and persistence, laughter and tears. In some, you'll hear the couples tell their stories themselves. In others, I'll step in to offer a pastor's view of what God was doing behind the scenes. While every story is true and drawn from real couples, a few details have been thoughtfully shaped to preserve the flow and heart of each account. My hope is that as you read, your faith will be stirred and your eyes opened to a God who is still near, still moving, and still writing new stories of His grace on both the mountaintop and in the valley of the shadow of death.

CHAPTER 1

The Shadow of Death

Even though I walk through the valley of the shadow of death,
I will fear no evil, for You are with me;
Your rod and Your staff, they comfort me.
> **PSALM 23:4 (ESV)**

KNOWING HOW A story will end doesn't make it any easier to watch, and it certainly doesn't make it any easier to experience. It was in 2015 that Alvin and Mizpah (Mitch) Bulahan were taken into the hideously beige office of their obstetrician and told that the baby they had just conceived had little chance of even surviving labor. The good doctor, gentle but practiced, brought out all sorts of charts and diagrams, carefully explaining that the Bulahans' little Matthew showed signs of a fatal genetic trisomy. As the doctor spoke, Mitch began to cry.

Alvin, on the other hand, a doctor himself, remained scarily still. He didn't look at the obstetrician. Instead, he stared past her at a plaque propped up on the bookshelf behind her desk.

"Dr. Alvin? Dr. Alvin—you still with me here?" The obstetrician spoke calmly, keeping her voice steady. In her decades-long career, such conversations hadn't yet gotten any easier. "Dr. Alvin?"

"Huh?" Alvin blinked.

"I know this is hard to hear, and you probably have questions. I just want to be sure—"

"Johns Hopkins."

"I'm sorry?"

"Johns Hopkins," he said again, pointing at the plaque. "Great school. A few of my friends went there."

"Oh. Y-yes. It is. I graduated in '95."

The doctor and Mitch looked at each other. Through tears, Mitch saw her husband's blank expression, his eyes looking almost through the doctor and at the bookshelf behind.

"Alvin, honey? Are you all right?"

"Perfectly." He turned to his wife, a weak smile on his lips, his eyes devoid of emotion.

"Dr. Alvin," the doctor tried again, "I just want to make sure that we all have a clear grasp on—"

"Trisomy 18. Edwards syndrome," Alvin interrupted. His voice was calm. Clinical. He had more than a firm grasp on the situation. "It disrupts development. Most cases end in miscarriage, stillbirth, or death shortly after birth. Everything's clear to me, Doctor. Matthew isn't going to make it."

Alvin still wasn't really looking at the doctor. Rather, he avoided her empathic gaze like making eye contact would somehow kill Matthew right there in the womb. Her compassion was too evident in her expression; her eyes said something too human. The words made sense. Nothing else did.

The room seemed to shrink. The wallpaper was more

nauseating now, the beige dirtier. It was quiet. No. Too loud. A million noises that Alvin had never paid attention to before now bombarded his senses. The electric hum of fluorescent box lights above him, the chugging of fax machines and printers in a room to their right, the metronomic ticking of the wall clock.

The doctor exchanged another glance with Mitch, then gently rose from her chair. "I'll give you two a moment."

Alvin dropped his head down and stared intently at the mud-brown carpet below him. He found himself mesmerized by the pattern. So simple, yet so intricate. Thousands of fibers, crisscrossing over one another, all working in tandem to create something that would only ever exist to be trampled underfoot by man.

"Alvin? Would you talk to me?" Mitch took Alvin's hand in hers and placed it on her lap. "Please?"

After what felt like an eternity of silence, Alvin responded. "We can't terminate." A single tear escaped his eye and fell, instantly vanishing into the carpet.

"We won't."

Alvin felt the ticking of the clock, the buzz of the lights, and the whir of machinery diminish as the sound of his breathing grew more powerful. His chest grew tighter, his heart grew heavier, and his eyes felt too weak to hold back the tears. Mitch wrapped her arms around him as he began to cry.

Alvin found Mizpah at a time when the prospect of her finding love again seemed to be a mere fantasy. After all, there aren't many men out there who would be willing to marry into the responsibility of four kids. They got married in 2014.

Alvin had wanted to be a father his whole life, and when he met Mitch and her children, he didn't see an unneeded burden in them, but the chance for him to experience the joy of fatherhood many times over. Of course, he kept his desire to father a child of his own, but he made it clear that even if that wasn't in the cards for them, he would stick by Mitch for as long he lived.

In 2015, Mitch got pregnant, but the excitement of a potential new sibling (for the kids) and a child of his own (for Alvin) was soon replaced with unimaginable grief when doctors said that Matthew wouldn't make it. Trisomy 18 is a rare genetic disorder where a baby develops an additional copy of chromosome 18. It almost always leads to severe developmental abnormalities and a range of birth defects. Many pregnancies end in miscarriage or stillbirth, and most infants who are born alive do not survive beyond their first year. Those who do survive face profound intellectual and developmental disabilities for the rest of their lives. This brings whole new meaning to the biblical metaphor used by the psalmist, *the shadow of death*. For the Bulahans, Matthew's life was marked by that shadow, that promise of death at some point in his first year.

Choosing not to terminate, the Bulahans endured the pregnancy, trying to live as normally as they could. They even threw a baby shower for Matthew, telling only a few about the story's inevitable conclusion. They decided to celebrate life as long as they could, despite knowing what was around the corner.

Matthew was delivered and passed away just a few hours later. In the months following his death, loss clouded every aspect of the Bulahans' home life. While the rest of the family was able to eventually settle into their new normal in the aftermath of tragedy, Mitch carried on, still lost in grief. She stayed home most days, quietly mourning their son. Several months later, a miscarriage landed like a cruel confirmation. It looked like having any more kids was, just as they feared, not in the cards. It was then that Mitch chanced upon something unexpected.

ALVIN

It's been a long day in the ER, which I guess is all that can be expected when the city is slowly turning white outside my window. Snowstorms bring accidents, falls, frostbite, and broken bones. Those bring patients. Most people, if they had known the weather was going to get this bad, would've just called in sick and stayed home. But you know how it is. When you're on call, you're on call.

Besides the patients, paperwork has been piling up for a few days, and my PA is taking a much-needed trip to Lake Harmony for the week. It's a deserved holiday. Diane's nothing if not efficient when she's in, but I've missed having her around to help keep the chaos organized.

I'm on break, sitting in the cafeteria, nursing a cup of coffee that always gets too lukewarm to drink. As I aimlessly stir the dark-brown battery acid in my mug, I let my thoughts drift to Mitch. I'm worried about her. I think she feels somehow responsible for what's happened, which is crazy, but I can't tell *her* that.

I think she feels that I regret marrying her. That I'm somehow angry with her about Matthew, about the miscarriage. She's older than I am, and I know how age tends to affect these things, but that doesn't mean I would resent her. How could I ever think that way?

I think the miscarriage was the killer, a real "kick someone when they're down" moment. It broke our family's heart, but with time, most of us have learned to move on in some way. The trouble is Mitch hasn't yet escaped that memory. Postpartum is no joke. She hasn't been driving or even leaving the house that much. I've been praying that somehow, something will get her excited about life again.

BZZT-BZZT. I quit stirring and pick up my phone. A notification from Mitch.

MITCH
You have GOT to watch this . . .

I click on the link, and a live feed from a local church pops up. Grace Church. I've never heard of this place before, but first impressions? I like what this preacher has to say. It's a nice message, though I'm not sure I'd commit to going there.

MITCH
Can we go here sometime? I think it'd be good for us. Good for the kids.

MITCH

I've been searching for something that speaks to me, something that makes me feel like hoping again. I've believed in God all my life, so the default place I go when I'm not sure how I'm feeling or what comes next has always been the church and His Word. But I'd be lying if I said those were helping much right now. Christian influencers and their "You Got This!" posts feel tired and unoriginal. The sermons I'm hearing wash over me completely. It's like drilling for oil in the desert, searching for a reason to even be optimistic. I know it's out there somewhere, buried under all that sand. It's just going to be some time before I hit it.

I know Alvin can empathize. Alvin's empathy is what drew me to him. I think it's good that it's so central to who he is. A doctor without empathy isn't one I'd trust, and the fact that he hasn't become desensitized to others' pain because of his career is a big reason why his patients love him so much. So believe me when I say, I *know* Alvin can empathize. I just don't know that he, or anyone else in his situation, could ever really know what it's like to watch the life you created inside your body wither away in hours.

Matthew was a part of me. He lived inside me, and he lived there longer than he ever did in the real world. In the womb, he was safe; in the womb, he was alive. Out here, I wasn't able to protect him. I couldn't keep him alive.

Creating life is plenty emotional on its own. Death brings its own flurry of confusing emotions. Just think what experiencing the overlap does to a person. I remember reading about the fault lines in California, the ones that cause all those earthquakes. Like tectonic plates, grinding up against each other, were those two familiar friends on that day in the hospital—life and death. The world crumbled around me as I watched them fight over my little boy, and the results were, at least for me, truly earthshaking.

So, forgive me if I'm not all that fun to talk to.

I walked past a day care the other day and stopped by the window just to watch the children play. I saw a little girl, maybe around three years old, working on a block tower, painstakingly choosing blocks that to anybody else would look identical to all the others.

With the clunky, purposeful movements of a toddler still working out the kinks in her motor skills, she built her tower. Would it be crazy to say I could see her vision? I could see where the thinner ones were meant to represent huge pillars and the heavier ones at the bottom stone foundations. I could even see the villagers, selling their wares inside the castle walls. The archers in the towers, the soldiers patrolling the walls.

What? My son had a medieval military phase.

Anyway, I watched her build this tower, love this tower, and grow to feel responsible for it despite its flaws. And believe me, it had its flaws.

And then I saw a boy in a dinosaur T-shirt, about the same age, stomp over. He was innocent in his own way, in that he was at an age at which some boys are easy to read. There's little deception in boys around then. Their emotions, their intentions, their actions are impulsive. I could see it in his face. He was going to knock down that girl's tower. In his mind, he wasn't even trying to be "bad." It's just that the idea popped into his mind, and so he would do it. Kids that age don't really see any other option till they're eventually taught otherwise.

With a gleeful laugh, he swung his arms and walked forward into the little girl's construction, sending the blocks tumbling to the floor. She looked at him, struggling to coordinate all of the emotions she was feeling. Rage, discomfort, fear, confusion, and most of all, pain for what she'd lost. The tower she'd seen grow block by block, like a genome . . . block by block.

While he lived, we were going back for regular ultrasounds, watching him form in the womb. Block by block, his genetic code was being written. Piece by piece, he came together. His head, his eyes, his mouth, his hands. We waited for him to be finished, and then, everything that had been built in him was toppled. A tower that was never meant to last. A tower that existed for a while only to be turned into rubble.

I know I'm brooding right now, but you're going to need to let me have this. Guess there's nothing left for me to do but waste away for another day, log back in to Facebook, and keep drilling for oil.

This past Tuesday, when I was home during the blizzard, I chanced upon a sermon that spoke to me in a way not many have before. I can't explain why, but something about it drew me to this place.

As we walked through the front doors of Grace Church, we were greeted by what felt like hundreds of people. Genuine smiles, warm hugs, and brotherly handshakes for Alvin and the boys. This was our first day here, and we already felt a little like family.

All I could think about through the whole service was how Alvin and the children felt about this place. I caught myself looking at them after every big moment during worship, after almost every line the pastor spoke, and in the lobby as we mingled with our . . . churchmates?

Can I call them that? Is it too soon, or is that the whole point? What is the church if not family? What are the elders there if not uncles, aunts, and grandparents you just happen not to be related to? What are youth there if not older siblings and cousins for our kids?

The kids. I want to go here, more for the kids than anything. They've already started making friends, and with the way everything's run, I know they'll appreciate it so much more than the old-school kind of church I've become comfortable with in my years as a pastor's daughter. I think Alvin likes this place too. He smiled almost the whole time, and he's smiling right now, in the car headed home.

This man was a gift from God to me. I don't know where I and the kids would've been without him. He's funny, intelligent, and a pure soul. He could be nothing less, as anyone without a heart made of gold would never do what he did for me and my family.

Plus, he isn't a pastor's son, which is a huge plus in my book.

I know he would never admit it, but I think he's still a little hurt that he'll never get to experience being a new parent. And it's all my fault. I pray every night that things will change, but I think it's time I accept they probably never will.

ALVIN

A few weeks ago, I told Mitch that if we were going to be part of this church, we should *be* part of this church. To me, that means going the distance: getting our kids involved, and then getting involved ourselves. A church is a family, and what good is a family that you barely see? A community is a family. What good is a family you barely get to know? In my worldview, going to church can never be a passive affair, and I know Mitch, as a pastor's daughter, understands better than I ever could. "Going to church" for her was a lifestyle, and we decided we'd love to have our kids accept just a little bit of that philosophy into their own lives. Day one of this so-called voyage to involvement, and we've already run aground.

Allow me to make something clear. We both agreed to start going to the Grace Church couples' group together last Sunday after hearing Pastor Courtney speak on it. Key words being *we both* and *agreed*. Now, we're arguing about it in the car parked outside the host's house.

"I don't know if this is a good idea, Alvin. Can't we just go home?" she says, looking away from me and at Pastor Courtney's front door.

"Come on, Mitch. We promised each other we'd go this week. We promised the pastor! Besides, we're already here—"

"And we could be gone in two seconds. All you have to do is flip that gear from neutral to drive and put your foot on the gas." She still isn't looking at me.

"What kind of example are we setting for the kids—"

"The kids are the only reason I came here! All I want is a place where the kids feel safe and are learning something. They like it here, Alvin! That's the only reason we're here."

"Really? The only reason?" I sigh and place my hand on hers. She's gripping the side of her seat like her life depends on it. Her hands are cold to the touch. "Mitch, you found this church. You said you liked what they had to say, and I agreed with you. I like it here. But, if we're gonna be here, we have to really *be* here."

She finally turns to look at me. I tell her that if she ends up hating it, we'll leave.

She's having a great time. Figures. I mean, I'm having a great time too, but man, does she make it seem like this whole thing was her idea. I've been watching her for the past hour, laughing it up with the other women here. A natural extravert when she gives herself the opportunity, Mitch is quick to make friends wherever she goes. In fact, I think she's already found a new *best* friend (if I'm not being too presumptuous), a woman named Monique.

A sharp *CLAP-CLAP* penetrates the ambient murmur of party chatter.

"Guys, I think it's getting around that time we start wrapping it up. Trust me, I'd love to have you all here for the night, but our daughter's got school in the morning."

I watch Pastor Courtney make his way to the center of the room.

"But before we go, I want to head into this next week with an attitude of gratitude. If we could all just go around and say something, even something small, that we're grateful for."

"Pastor Courtney, if I could?" Somehow, my wife has just *appeared* next to the pastor.

He nods to her.

"Hey, everybody. If we haven't met yet, my name's Mitch. Over there is my husband, Alvin. I think I speak for both of us when I say that what we're most thankful for tonight is all of you."

What we're most thankful for is all of you . . .

She has a habit of making everything feel like it was her idea. Given her extraversion and my being caught off guard, it probably looked like she dragged me in here and not the other way around! I'm not complaining, though. I'm just barely holding back my excitement. All I wanted was for her to have a good time, and she did.

MITCH

There are those that you take some time to get comfortable with and those you seem to connect with instantly. Monique belonged to the second group. Within minutes of meeting at that couples' group, we were laughing and joking like old friends. We found out we had a lot in common. Some of those things were nice and wholesome, like our tastes in music and restaurants we like. I found out that day that we also had another thing in common, and it relates to an experience that I wouldn't wish upon my worst enemy.

I drove to ladies' Bible study today. Yes, I *drove*. You should've seen Alvin's face when I came downstairs this morning, Bible in hand and asking for the car keys. He was equal parts shocked and over the moon.

When I got here, I found my friend and stuck by her for most of the day. The Bible study ended a while back, but Monique and I are still in the empty sanctuary while the others talk in the lobby. I was glad I'd found a partner in my grief, someone who understood, but the result of our meeting was a multiplying of that grief. Two souls who'd lost everything, sitting in that emptiness together. The pain grew almost exponentially, and it wasn't either of our faults. I think there's something about the shared sorrow we felt that drew us to each other, and I'm not surprised that, having had time to sit with it, both of us discovered that we weren't nearly as far along in recovery as we'd thought.

As much as we've tried to move past it, we haven't been able to lose that sinking feeling that neither of us will ever mother a child again. I don't know that I'd ever want to say it out loud, but there's a part of me that thinks a lot of my self-worth rides on this. It doesn't make any sense, I know. It's not like I haven't mothered a small army already, but that's just it. I've experienced new parenthood many times over. I've experienced many "first days" of preschool and several "first words." I've changed diapers and groaned at being woken up at three in the morning by their cries. Most importantly, many times over, I've experienced actually bringing home a living newborn from the hospital. Something so simple and necessary for all those other joys in life, and Alvin might never experience it. What was his crime? That we found each other too late in life?

Monique listened to me rant with understanding in her eyes. I realized as I was talking to her that she's the only one in a long time that I'd uttered these words to: "I want to have another baby."

I'd been avoiding saying the words, like they would be an insult to our Matthew. What kind of mother was I, that I'd want to replace him so soon? What kind of woman am I if I can't? It's an unhealthy place to go, but I can't help going there.

We're sitting in the empty sanctuary, holding each other, when we see Pastor Alicia excuse herself from a conversation in the lobby and walk toward us.

"Mitch? Monique? What's going on?"

Oh no. I can feel myself getting ready to blurt it out. I can feel it coming up, like acid in my throat, and I'm trying to hold it back. I'm going to tell her what's wrong, and truthfully, what's wrong is the fact that I want to have a baby. The tears are fighting at the back of my eyelids now. Just like that, the levee breaks.

I'm going to tell her. I'm going to tell her that I want a baby. What that's going to do for me now, I do not know.

ALVIN

Complications. I hate that word. We use it all the time to describe things that are actually pretty simple. Humans aren't complicated, and neither are the things that happen to us. We're simple creatures, and the simple truth is that right now, I'm afraid.

Let me backtrack a little bit. Mitch and Monique were both prayed over after a conversation with Pastor Alicia (Pastor Joe's wife). I'd been driving home from work, just passing by the church, when she texted me:

> MITCH
> *come to the church, pls.*

My mind immediately went to car trouble. But then:

> MITCH
> *The pastor wants to pray for us.*

Matthew.

Why my mind went there next, to this day, I could not tell you. Pastors pray. It's what they do. Why then did I immediately think of Matthew?

> MITCH
> *I was talking about our baby.*

Our baby? The one we'd lost? Or was it possible that . . .

MITCH

Pls come if you can.

Hope.

I wasted no time in taking a quick detour to join them inside, and Mitch quickly brought me up to speed. Pastor Alicia had said that she would go and get her husband, which felt a bit strange considering it came right after my wife had said, "I'm having trouble getting pregnant." You'll have to forgive my initial shock, but I don't think it was completely unwarranted. For a split second, I wondered, *Oh no, exactly what kind of church is this?*

I didn't know it at the time, but apparently, over the years, he'd unintentionally developed an unofficial title: "the baby pastor." He walked out of the office and into the sanctuary, joining us where we were standing in front of the altar.

It was surreal, truly, when he came over and prayed one of the simplest prayers I've ever heard. He asked us about Matthew, and if we were absolutely sure that another child is what we wanted most in this life. Then, he spoke to Monique. He placed his hands on the shoulders of both women and with conviction, said these four words: "It's a done deal."

We didn't feel any different, and maybe we were wrong to expect that we would. When God moves in the modern world, it's oftentimes a lot less "Ten Commandments" and a lot more as the "still, small voice." I'm a doctor, trained to be skeptical, but a few months later, Mitch got pregnant. I can only describe that as miraculous.

It was difficult to contain our shock and obvious joy, but tragedy has a way of coloring your perspective. Miscarriage and early neonatal loss have a unique ability to breed a "once-bitten" mentality, and that kept us from fully enjoying Mitch's completely unlikely pregnancy. We covered our bases, but still slept little. We decided not to tell anyone out of fear that this might end up like . . . well. So far, so good.

But then, last week, Mitch bled. I was in the kitchen, pouring myself a bowl of cereal when she came in and told me. She came in and told me that she'd found blood. You should've seen how the color just drained from my face.

That whole thing turned out to be a false alarm, but life sure has a sick sense of humor sometimes. Then, as if to kick a man when he's down, this week, a routine prenatal examination revealed signs of "cervical insufficiency." Also known as having an "incompetent cervix." Put basically, Mitch's cervical muscles are weakening, and if we weren't careful—I'm sure you can guess by this point.

She's been taking it easy all week, on the doctor's orders and mine. She's not a fan of the bed rest, but we couldn't take any chances. Tonight, I'm sitting with her in our room. She's reclined on the bed, and I'm at our desk, scouring medical journals.

"Alvin? Would you please come to bed?" she asks. "It's late."

"I'm not tired," I respond dryly, even though I'm tired out of my mind. Like I said, neither of us have been sleeping much. I'm not sure how Mitch has been staying so calm. I fully expected her to be a wreck.

"I know it's scary—"

"I'm not afraid. I'm just trying to understand as much about what's happening right now as I can." Understanding means familiarity. Understanding means safety.

"It's not a bad thing to say you're feeling afraid, you know."

"When has saying they're afraid ever helped anyone?" I get up from my desk and sit beside Mitch on the edge of our mattress.

"It helped me." She takes my hand. "We only have this baby because I went to someone and told them exactly what I was afraid of. I was afraid we might never have this opportunity, that you might never experience what it means to be a father from the very start of someone's life. I said all this, out loud, to another human being. Then she brought me to her husband. He said it's a done deal, and I believe him."

"It's not that I don't believe—"

"But what's happening is bringing back memories of—"

"Yeah."

"I've been thinking about him a lot too. He hasn't left my mind since the day I bled."

I'll admit, I'm more than taken aback by her calmness in all this. After all, it was she who knew better than anyone just how terrifying this could be. After Matthew, she didn't smile for months, leave the house, or speak to her friends. Even her words to me were sometimes few and far between. Now she's sitting here, with admittedly more to lose from another miscarriage, consoling me? Telling me not to worry? Telling me not to be afraid? I'm confused and desperate to ask a question that feels almost too basic. But I'm watching somebody who I knew when they were truly broken now walking, talking, and acting like a completely new person.

"Mitch, I . . . how? How can you not be afraid?"

"I am," she responds, gently resting her palm on my cheek. Clearly, I'd missed something.

"Believe me, I am. But if there's anything I've learned from this new family it's that saying so is the difference between letting it have power over you and being totally free."

MITCH

"I feel like it's been so long since we've gotten together," says Grace, taking a sip of tea.

"Too long," I reply. Grace is one of my oldest friends. We grew up on the same street and went to the same church (my dad's) all our lives. Before coming to Grace Church, Alvin and I had been extremely involved in her husband's New Brunswick church plant. I've always been able to relate to the struggle of building up a church from nothing. After all, I watched my father fight that battle for years. Even though our family has a new church to call home now, we still try to stay in contact and swing by for any events happening at Grace's.

"I'm sorry I haven't been around to see you till now. Things have been a little crazy." Grace looks down at the floor. "But you have no idea how excited I've been for you. I'm sure the kids are too."

I don't blame Grace for not reaching out as much. I'm sure the pressures of church planting (the least of which are financial) haven't been easy on her and her husband. "Don't apologize for having a lot on your plate, Grace. You're gonna make me feel bad. And yeah, the kids are over the moon. They've even voted on a name."

"Oh, really?" Grace's face grows brighter. "You got the little rascals to reach a consensus on something?"

"Surprisingly easier than I thought it would be."

"C'mon, walk me through the process. How'd they decide?"

"For starters, she definitely has to have an *M* name."

"Of course."

"And from there, Alvin and I gave the kids a week to brainstorm and bring us their three favorites. They ended up just bringing us one, and we loved it." I look down and stir my coffee, realizing this will be the first time I've told this to anybody.

"You're killing me here, Mitch. What'd you guys pick?"

Suddenly, I feel like the name needs something more. Sitting in front of me was Grace, a woman to whom I wasn't giving enough credit. After Alvin and the kids, her voice was the first one I turned to after Matthew had passed. Going back even further, she and her husband were the only ones who knew how his story was going to end before it did. At the baby shower we threw for Matthew, she stood by me as I was approached by couple after couple coming to offer their congratulations. She would periodically squeeze my hand to calm the tremors. Without her, I might've just broken down right there. I spoke to her almost every day for the few months after we lost him when I was too anxious to drive or even step out of the house. She'd been a busy woman back then, too, but she didn't hesitate to live up to her namesake: Grace. Funny coincidence that the place where Alvin and I learned to believe again would share the same name.

"Mitch? Are you okay?"

"Huh? Oh, sorry."

"That's okay," Grace says with a laugh. "So . . . a name?"

"Grace."

"Yeah?"

"Marceline Grace."

ALVIN

If there are speed limits posted around here, I'm driving way too fast to see them. The world outside my window is made up of nothing more than blurred shades of green and gray as I barrel down these rough mountain roads. *Go to the men's retreat,* she said. *I'll be fine,* she said.

I drove down this morning with Jay, another member of the men's group. It was nice. The hour-and-a-half drive into the mountains was scenic. We got to our cabin while most of the guys were already at breakfast, unloaded our stuff, and bummed around till our afternoon seminar. The whole day was spent swapping stories, arguing about Brady's status as the greatest of all time (which got way harder for guys like me after Super Bowl LI), and eating. A lot. I regret that now because my stomach is churning as I'm racing home to Mitch at one-thirty in the morning.

The past few weeks haven't been the greatest, with her developing symptoms of preeclampsia. If it's really that that she's developing, this is beyond serious. Preeclampsia is a condition characterized by a high blood pressure and even potential organ damage. It's a leading cause of maternal and infant death. I know that most mothers who develop this complication do end up recovering and delivering healthy babies, but there is a percentage that doesn't. There's a percentage that develops eclampsia (when a woman with preeclampsia experiences seizures or loses consciousness). There's a percentage that dies.

Now, there's no guarantee Mitch even has preeclampsia. She's been feeling ill, having headaches and blurred vision. I didn't really want to go to the retreat with her in this condition, but she wouldn't have it. She told me to go, and I did, and now I think she's in labor. Thirty-seven weeks in, November 5, 2017, and the baby is coming.

MITCH

She's here, and she made quite the entrance. She was born facing the ceiling, which from experience, I can tell you, is rare. I know that's a fun fact Alvin is going to want to tell everyone. It's a surreal feeling, being back in this kind of bed and in this kind of room after so long. The last time I was in a position like this . . .

At first, when I awoke, the surgical white of my bedsheets and the hum of the medical equipment was nauseating. They all brought me back to the last time I was in this building, giving birth to a child I knew wouldn't live. I remember how we tried our hardest to pretend like everything was normal. I remember Alvin posting Matthew on Facebook, only to have his doctor friends instantly ask why the baby didn't look well. I remember how the kids doted over Matthew, cherishing him for the time they knew was limited. The pain of those memories will never fully disappear, but I can feel the power they had on our lives melting away.

I hear the shuffling of what feels like a hundred pairs of feet in the hallway outside my room. I'm not surprised. I always knew she'd be a celebrity.

ALVIN

"Everybody, come on in! Everybody gets to hold the baby!"

I think I've turned this floor of the hospital into a madhouse, but I honestly do not care. Dozens of our friends, family, and churchmates turned up at the hospital at my invitation, and Mitch and I could not be happier for it. I've ordered a truckload of pizza, which should be getting here any minute.

It doesn't get much better than this. Marcy is soaking up the attention from her older siblings at the right end of the couch. My wife is half asleep to my left. On the TV is a rerun of one of my all-time favorite movies: *It's a Wonderful Life*. The fireplace is crackling, and tomorrow's a Saturday. I could die happy right now.

It's been almost a year since Marcy was born, and not to sound cliche, but I don't know if I'm the same man I was before she came. Experiences like the one I had last year have a way of putting things into perspective. You realize how good God is to you, and you start regretting those moments that feel like wasted time. Every time I hold Marcy is a reminder of a unique blessing that I don't deserve, and now I can't help but feel that there's more I could be doing to get closer to God.

Am I being cognizant of who I am in God? Is everything I'm doing glorifying Him? Is everything I'm doing productive or bringing me closer to a goal? Sorry to get totally existential on you all, but these are the things that have been on my mind lately. I've always loved to learn. I kind of have to for the profession I chose. I've been trying to apply that thirst for knowledge to God's Word in order to understand, on a deeper level, what is contained between the covers of the Holy Bible. When you study with passion, you'll be surprised by what God reveals to you.

I can't waste time. It's precious. I know what a gift I've been given in my life, my family, and now Marceline. That's why I can't help but try to draw closer to my God, and in the process, become the kind of man my wife can depend on and all my children can look up to.

Conclusion
What's Not Revealed . . .

Anyone who watched the interviews we conducted for this book knows that these stories make me emotional—and I'm proud of that. I think it's a good thing. The way I see it, my personal investment in each of these couples' lives only makes this whole project more worth it. Why write a book about something that doesn't move *you* first and foremost? I love sharing stories, in my writing or in sermons, because I believe in their ability to be more personally impactful than just empirical data or theory. Christ used parables, the greatest apostles and teachers related complex ideas with simple analogies, and while I don't claim that a single one of these stories could ever attain "parable status," I don't think they're empty of deeper meaning. Stories, in good taste, can have immeasurable teaching power. My hope is to convince you of that fact through the rest of your reading, but for right now, let's begin with a few things that instantly stick out to me from the Bulahans' story.

We see a beautiful example of one of my personal philosophies working at its best. I always say: "What's not revealed can't be healed." It's this idea that gives Mitch a renewed perspective on life when Alvin struggles to ease his anxieties. Her breakthrough didn't come from ignoring her fear or attempting to "understand" her way out of it, but from admitting the fact that it was real.

Don't get me wrong. Understanding what we fear is a part of revealing it. A good voice in your life doesn't see you afraid and say, "But God says, 'Be not afraid!'" That's unhelpful. That's impractical. When you were a kid and scared of the dark, on some level, defeating that fear meant addressing that fact that you weren't scared of the dark exactly, but what could be in that space you couldn't fully see.

Negative emotions only have power over you as long as you try to avoid facing them. They're like monsters in your room that you spend your whole childhood trying to hide from. You avoid looking in the closet at night in case a pile of clothes turns into the bogeyman right before your eyes. You bury yourself in the covers so that if something does emerge from that dark closet, it won't see you.

Now take that logic and apply it to the very real dangers of life. Jesus invites us to join Him in a life free of worry that's totally dependent on God. We're told to cast our burdens upon Him because He cares for us. For Him to carry our burdens, we must admit the existence of said burdens to begin with. This is key, and as can be seen from the Bulahans' personal testimony, this method works. What isn't revealed has no chance of being healed, which is why we work extremely hard to foster an atmosphere in which people are comfortable being vulnerable. The internal monologues of Mitch and Alvin were our modest attempt to put the complexity of people to paper. The contradictory, mind-twisting way that our feelings prey on our spirits is very real, and as we saw, the pressure builds till it's ideally released in a community you can trust. Notice how I said *trust*! I want to emphasize that because I know a lot of us have made the mistake of opening up around people we shouldn't. Around those people, being vulnerable can be like diving into a shark tank with a paper cut. In those circles, all your vulnerability is blood in the water. I know it sounds dark, but I speak confidently with the knowledge that we've all probably experienced this at least once. I have, and I've been burned. It takes a while to want to be vulnerable with people after that.

In the Bulahans' case, while there isn't specifically a time when they'd been "burned" for their vulnerability, Mitch specifically struggled because she'd come to a point when wanting and hoping felt too dangerous. Dangerous enough in her own mind, and ten times more dangerous when those wants were verbalized. I know a lot of people who've admitted to feeling this way as well. We live in a culture of unrealized dreams. Every day the world seems to get worse. People don't want to have kids because they don't see a purpose in the life they live. They don't see anything worthwhile in the world they'd be bringing kids into. The Bulahans feared because they'd already gotten so close to something they wanted so badly, only for it to be ripped away. In a culture of despair, simply being honest enough to say "I want" feels like a luxury most people can't afford. It's for all these reasons that I say this: People's vulnerability is a gift—it means they trust you. It's a great honor to know that people feel ready to share some of the worst parts of themselves and their lives with you, and I've experienced enough to know that bringing those things to light is the only way they truly get resolved. We saw that in an extremely literal sense when Mitch worked up the courage to say, "I want another baby." She realized an inner longing for another baby, and she received. It sounds simple and straightforward when I say it like that, but "straightforward" isn't part of the equation of real life. The trauma I experienced all through my life didn't get miraculously resolved in one magical church service.

As those of you who read my other book know, bad habits and scars both have a way of taking a while to be rid of. For instance, let's take addiction. I continued doing cocaine well into my first few years as a Christian. I hated myself for it, and it's true that I wasn't using nearly as much as I was in my BC era, but I was still a weekend warrior that needed the occasional fix.

It took my wife finding out and threatening to expose me to the church leadership that finally shocked me into action. In one church staff meeting, I remember breaking down in tears, sobbing as I confessed, "I'm doing cocaine!" It's a very dramatic example, but it perfectly demonstrates what I'm trying to get across to you. What's not revealed can't be healed. I was forced to reveal something I'd been keeping hidden, and pushing it into the light was the step of faith I needed to take in order for it to be addressed.

Whatever You Celebrate

I remember praying for Monique and Mitch. My wife came and got me from my office, saying that two women had recently miscarried and were looking to get pregnant. I prayed for them both, declaring that "it" was done. There was no doubt in my mind that they would both have kids in due time.

However, an unexpected hurdle was that Monique got pregnant before Mitch did. With twins too! Around the same time, several women in our church announced their pregnancies, and poor Mitch was left with nothing but negative tests. That was especially trying for me. Of course, I believed entirely that Mitch would have her baby soon enough, but I couldn't help but feel bad for her as she watched all of her closest friends speed ahead in life. It's not just the wait that can kill you, but the squeeze, the crushing, the pressing . . .

These kinds of curveballs have the potential to really diminish your faith, but Mitch was a picture of sainthood through these especially rough months. She was brimming with joy and doted on each of her friends and their children like they were her own. She didn't become anxious or jealous, even though she was still waiting for the blessing they had already received.

I'm reminded of a similar situation involving my own daughters. When Jacqui announced that she was pregnant, I was overjoyed, but I felt for her older sister Alex. She was older, she'd been waiting. *What about her?* The worry gnawed at the back of my mind. It's only human to feel this way, but an hour later, that conflicted mess of feelings turned to pure ecstasy when Alex announced that she was also pregnant. Purely a coincidence that they'd both planned on revealing their pregnancies at the same time, but it sure makes for a good story.

Mitch celebrated each one of her friends' blessings like they were her own. She didn't become jealous or frustrated with God, that the people around her could no longer relate to her struggle. She wasn't bitter that even Monique, someone who got prayed over alongside her, got pregnant with twins before she saw a single shred of evidence that God planned to come through for her.

This is something I say almost every week: "Whatever you celebrate, you will appropriate." My goal with this phraseology isn't to raise Christians who are over-obsessed with material blessings, or "manifesting" them into existence, but to remind them to celebrate the good things in life, and in Mitch's case, that meant her friends' children. In a culture obsessed with personal gain and pulling down others in order to get ahead, it's something completely radical to say that if we don't celebrate the blessings we see in the lives of others, we are impeding our ability to take hold of our own (or recognize them when they come, because we've become so fixated on what others have already gotten). If Mitch had wavered in her faith or grown bitter, who knows if her even having a baby would've fixed the irreparable damage to her soul. When we see others being blessed with something we feel should be rightfully ours, it's easy to grow resentful of God and people. Mitch didn't, and a blessing for her family soon followed.

Seven Years

The LORD is near to the brokenhearted and saves the crushed in spirit.

PSALM 34:18 (ESV)

Is It Over?

WHEN I FIRST met Marcela many years ago, something about the way she carried herself reminded me of my own story. In her eyes I could see a quiet grit forged by years of practiced resilience. Resilient people are admired, but few realize that their stoic determination and thick skin often come at a heavy cost. I sensed in her the same dogged intensity I learned to lean on during my roughest years. This wouldn't have been notice-able in her expression to many people, but I've always been able to sense the burdens of those who've lived lives like mine. People who've fought against the tide and are well acquainted with tragedy. People who've felt truly *alone*. That shared tenacity and stubbornness have carried people like us our whole lives, and would carry Marcela through seven years of ups, downs, and surprising moments of grace.

Let me back up a little bit. Born and raised in Ecuador, Marcela lost her parents when they passed away in her teens. Soon after, she became a victim of the system. She bounced around orphanages and less-than-optimal foster homes, and it was here that Marcela first met true loneliness—that feeling of being entirely on your own even while surrounded by people. She grew comfortable in the constant noise of her world when it rained, as the incessant pattering on thin, tin roofs drowned out the crashes of liquor bottles smashing and the sounds of her playing siblings. Both domestic anger and joy were alike to her at this time. She lived in homes filled with people, but truly knew none of them. This is what it's like to be fully numb. In numbness, Marcela moved forward, and around the time she finished high school, she moved to America.

She figured that she had left her misfortune behind, screaming and belligerent on the shores of Ecuador, furious at her escape from his slimy hand. Here, in the famed land of opportunity, she was convinced that her luck would turn around. She had manufactured an expectation of American suburbia in her mind. Holidays and family meals reminiscent of Rockwell's paintings. Streets paved with gold and a land flowing with milk and honey. To the huddled masses of the world, yearning to break free, simply stepping foot in America is expected to come with an answer to everything. Don't get me wrong; the gift of a new environment, especially the one here in the States, can do a lot. But provide a way out of the loneliness that had defined Marcela's life? That, Lady Liberty was not prepared to do. That's what we call a "God problem." Just when it felt like things might be looking up, her guardian succumbed to multiple sclerosis, leaving Marcela alone at age nineteen in an unfamiliar country.

In many ways, she didn't much miss out on some quintessential American traditions. Prom? Homecoming? High school football and tailgating? A comfortable life in a nuclear family? These things slipped under the radar, sure. But 2:00 a.m. shifts at the diner, being verbally abused by unruly customers all for a mediocre paycheck that's only going to pay for a college education? Now, that's what I call the "pick-yourself-up-by-the-bootstraps" special. There is scarcely anything more American than the sheer persistence needed to do what Marcela did. Nothing captures the heart of the American dream like Marcela's single-sighted fixation on a goal. That's a deeply American experience that a few of us unfortunate souls can relate to, but Lord knows, those of us who've managed to tap into the good life from the struggle we were born into wouldn't have traded those years of exhaustion and hustling for anything.

Marcela worked several jobs to put herself through college, all the while numbing her inner confusion with whatever felt appropriate at the time. In your twenties, the club is the only thing that feels appropriate, so Marcela was often found with her girlfriends at various discotheques around New Jersey (most of which I frequented myself in my BC era). It was at one such hotspot that she met the man who would become her husband: Alessandro, an Italian from Naples. Their meeting felt almost God-ordained, seeing as they came from completely opposite sides of the planet. The two eventually got married. Marcela began working for an online direct sales firm, and Alessandro found success as a restaurateur. And so began the seven years' war . . .

Year one. Her friends began settling down and starting families of their own. Every baby shower, every first birthday party. It all bit into her confidence. When women crowded around, raving about the glowing moms-to-be, Marcela's forced smile nearly cracked. She had been trying for a year, and while neither Marcela nor her husband had even uttered the word *infertile*, she was beginning to wonder if it was a possibility. But, no matter. *For some women, it just takes a little longer . . . right?*

Year three. More weddings, more baby showers, more first birthdays. The kids that had been born in their first year of trying were now beginning to talk and walk. How cute. Their development so perfectly complemented the tragically impressive collection of negative tests Marcela was building. A whispered "maybe next month" to Alessandro in the dark. A flutter of hope when she was late. But each month bled into the next. At this point, she had been trying long and consistently enough to be labeled as infertile.

Year five. When they first got married, they had begun eyeing schools. They'd even thought about moving into a larger house. One with a bigger yard for children to play in and maybe even a sturdy oak for a tree house. They'd started saving up for a down payment in their second year of trying, but now, nearing their sixth, they had probably saved enough to pay it off. But the money sat with no kids to spend it on. That fantasy of giving your kids everything you wished you could've had is real, but the chances of that fantasy being realized had long since slipped out of mind. They continued to try, almost as an obligation.

I don't think I have to tell you that seven years is a long time to try for a kid with no luck. Generally, a year is enough to get someone declared medically infertile. Seven years of negative tests. Seven years of shattered hopes. Seven years of trying—no one would blame them for simply giving up.

But there's that resilience I mentioned earlier showing itself. A headstrong determination that pursues desire. After feeling the void of familial love for so long, Marcela simply wasn't ready to accept that she would never be able to have a child of her own. The doctors explained to the couple that without IVF, a pregnancy would likely not be possible.

The pair traveled to Ecuador for the treatment. It cost $40,000, not counting their stay or travel expenses. That is a truly shocking amount of money, and people who don't understand the position this couple was in wouldn't be able to justify it in their heads. What could compel someone to fork out tens of thousands of dollars for a *chance*? Was it worth the gamble? Yes. To anybody who has the resources to support children and has wanted them all their lives but has been denied even a single natural pregnancy, this was more than worth it. I'm not saying that I'd recommend it, but I can't fully knock the value they put on having kids of their own. I can't just write off their willingness to pay as frivolous spending. Everyone needs that thing. That one thing that makes you just a little crazy. That one thing you'd risk it all for.

Marcela was uncomfortable with the idea at first, feeling like she was "playing God." When life itself is already so mysterious, creating it in a laboratory feels alien. It's not that she thought that those who accepted IVF treatment were somehow less than those who conceived completely naturally. Some of her friends had done it. In fact, it was some of those very friends who encouraged her to take the step. It's just that this IVF question forced her and Alessandro, both coming from historically conservative countries on the topic, to wrestle with what it truly meant to be a mother or a father. Intercourse, impregnation, birth, parenthood. Did life in this century necessarily have to develop in this exact order and this order alone? Is adoption or IVF or anything else that moved out of this preestablished order somehow wrong? Marcela and Alessandro fought with and among themselves. *Are we defying God or partnering with Him?* In their desperation, they decided that being a worthy father or mother wasn't restricted to just one format. There were those who couldn't conceive at all that were better parents than those that could. Many men have been incredibly fertile in a natural sense, but worthless fathers as their "fertility" left strings of single mothers and broken families in their wake.

In the endocrinologist's office, the smell of antiseptic assaulted the couple's noses. Was it the muggy, tropical heat that was to blame for how much they were sweating in the sparsely decorated office or anxiety? Would this day be able to withstand the burden of great expectations and the thousands of dollars that went into making it possible?

To almost everyone's surprise, the treatment worked. She got pregnant! When she was cleared to leave, they hopped on a plane and headed back for the States. As they soared over the Atlantic, telltale bleeding alerted Marcela that something had gone terribly wrong. She clutched the armrest, feeling life spill out of her. Alessandro began to desperately pray under his breath, prayers taught to him when he was a boy. Passengers around them hushed and began to stare, alarmed by Marcela's tense, unnatural breathing. A miscarriage. Their final gamble, a desperate swing for the fences and it seemed they had struck out.

People always say the wrong things. Her family and friends offered little comfort. This wasn't something she could just "let go" of or "move on" from. This wasn't the time for a "life goes on" speech. This had been their last attempt, one they had made after much prayer and deliberation.

Frustrations rose. The couple grew irritated and weary, unsure of if they would continue or try again. For Marcela, nothing compared to the pain of that miscarriage. Not the loss or loneliness that had defined her whole life. Nothing could surpass the pain of feeling their baby simply cease to exist within her, thousands of feet above the ground.

Does God Love Me?

It was a rainy summer Sunday at Grace Church. I remember watching Marcela sit in the back, shoulders tense, mouthing the words of our worship songs. In her eyes, I saw the same question I once carried (and sometimes still do) in seasons of doubt and waiting: "Does God still see me?"

When I began announcing the upcoming baptism service, something shifted in the room and her expression. Tension between fear and hope. I shared how, after years of battling my own doubts, I'd finally stepped into the baptismal waters not because I'd "arrived" as a Christian, but because I was done carrying the weight of feeling uncertain on my own. I spoke about God's grace, the kind that chases after the worst of sinners like me. I glanced periodically at Marcela, and I could see her toying with the same decision I'd faced all those years ago.

She was at a crossroads. She would either give up on a God who seems to have given up on her or dive deeper into faith. She realized that despite having followed God for years, she had never taken the step to symbolize complete commitment to this life through baptism. By the time I invited anybody who felt ready to go "all in" to sign up, I could see that she'd made her decision. To her, this wasn't about just symbolizing faith, but clinging to it.

By this point, I had already prayed for her and continued to do so through her whole ordeal. I had placed my hand on her shoulder and told her as I had everyone else that this was a "done deal." There was no doubt in my mind that she would conceive eventually, but that doesn't mean it was easy watching her struggle. I would often see her crying at the altar and head over just to remind her that it was going to be okay. She knew about the "done deal." She knew about "having faith" and "trusting in God" and all the Christian-ese I could think to spout in that moment. So, instead of doing any of that, I just stood with her. Sometimes, people need you more than they need your words.

Marcela got baptized and decided that "giving up" was not in her vocabulary. Reflecting on that time now, she realizes that her behavior was a little frenzied, to say the least. At worst, she was downright insane. She began making plans with her husband to put together money for another IVF attempt, one in the US that would run them upward of fifty grand. Nobody seemed to understand just why this was so important to her, and it was only years later that she really understood it herself. She had never felt loved, and in her mind, a baby would fix that.

All her life she had felt alone, unloved to a degree. This creates a void in the soul, one that we try to fill with things of the world. For some, it's money, and for others it's alcohol. She had a husband who loved her, yes, but the human mind can be funny that way. It has an amazing ability to ignore everything and fixate on what it has decided is the "ultimate solution." The list of potential "ultimate solutions" is endless. In Marcela's case, a baby seemed to be the only thing that could replace the love she had lost. She would later come to realize that this void was the God-shaped vacuum in every human soul, one that can only be completely filled by the love of a Heavenly Father. However, although she knew on a surface level that God loved her, she had never felt truly cared for by Him. As it turns out, this is a feeling shared by most Christians.

On the first Sunday of 2019, I remember asking the church during a particular altar call to approach the front if they had never felt unconditionally loved by God. An unusual request, I know. I half expected crickets, and I don't think that was too wild an expectation on my part. I mean, would you as a pastor expect anything else when you ask a room full of longtime Christians if they've ever felt loved by God? Of course they have! That's why they're Christians, aren't they? What exactly would be the point of a God who is love, whose love you don't feel?

But, to my and Marcela's absolute shock, almost the entire congregation made their way forward. Hundreds. Hundreds of "Christians" who'd lived almost their entire lives with crosses around their necks and Bible verses on their Facebook, but who hadn't experienced what it truly meant to be loved. It's only then that the two of us understood just how much people were missing out on a relationship with God. In Marcela's case, it was simply admitting this that unlocked everything.

It was an epiphany, crashing over her in waves. At that moment, she realized that she wanted something good for bad reasons. She couldn't burden a newborn with the responsibility of filling some personal void of her own. How was that fair? Deep-seated issues wouldn't go away through motherhood. In fact, they would probably be amplified and passed down to an innocent new life that had nothing to do with anything.

Too often we want our possessions, accomplishments, families, or significant others to "fix" us. *If I just had a girlfriend, or money, or that new car, or a baby . . . then my life would be perfect.* We trick ourselves into thinking that our personal problems can be solved by the addition of just "one more thing." Unfortunately, that comes at a huge cost, one that *you* might not always have to deal with. No, when you make fallible humans your "ultimate solution," you're almost always going to be let down, and that pain will only transfer over to those people who never asked to be in that position. There are certain wounds only God can heal.

We all have that "one thing." But any "one thing" we expect to bring our lives meaning has the potential to disappoint. The challenge of believing in God is to make Him your "one thing."

I'm not saying it's easy. How does something as intangible as the love of God become the one thing we seek? Well, consistency in our spiritual walk is one thing, but so is self-awareness.

We can't know God fully till we find out what it is that we're replacing Him with. I look to the example of Moses, who asked desperately just to get a glimpse of His face. I look to David, who writes that the one thing he desires and seeks is to live with God all his life and spend his days caught up in His presence. These might seem like the ravings of frilly, head-in-the-clouds romantic types, but I promise you that there's something real to this. Something we can all pull from. If you've ever chased a cure in the wrong place, if you've ever given it all to something that didn't satisfy, if you've ever wondered if there was anything out there that cared if you lived or died . . . you know Marcela's story.

A feeling like a warm hug accompanied with a peace that made no sense enveloped Marcela. For the first time, God's unconditional love and peace became *real* things in her life. *So this is what it feels like to be free,* she thought to herself. *Maybe I don't need a baby. Maybe this is all I've ever really needed.*

Later that week, she walked into a clinic with a check in her hand. They had already scheduled the appointment, but Marcela didn't feel the usual anxiety. If this worked, she would be over the moon. If it didn't, she knew she would be okay.

While getting her preliminary blood tests done, the doctors discovered something highly unusual. Turns out she could take that check right on home.

The Rock of Ages

The devil doesn't leave you alone. The first four months of Marcela's pregnancy were riddled with nightmares of miscarriages and constant panic attacks. *You're gonna lose the baby,* was the lie of choice for the enemy during this season. *You. You will lose this baby.*

Although she couldn't really enjoy her pregnancy, she was persistent in her faith as she had been persistent with everything else in her life. She was up at the altar for prayer every Sunday without fail. Every time I saw her, I would try to offer a small word of encouragement. I remember thinking, *If Marcela can stand in faith week after week at that altar, so can we all.*

Through that season, she was reminded of how she first came to Christ. As a little girl, she watched her mother and father's relationship deteriorate. She watched her mother hit rock bottom, only to be lifted back up by God. In the final years of her life, Marcela's mother found religion and was revitalized by faith. She found community and a reason to live through the love of the Father. Marcela, as a young woman, saw how much this "Jesus guy" had transformed her mother's entire way of life. That left an impact, one that would be important as she found her own way.

When Christ is your foundation, hitting rock bottom only means that you've drawn nearer to where your help comes from. As Charles Spurgeon put it, "I have learned to kiss the waves that throw me up against the Rock of Ages." Marcela is not shy of shouting this from the rooftops: "I only made it through because my lowest moments brought me nearer to my God."

The doctors said that Lorenzo, her little boy, would be born with a slew of serious complications. His umbilical cord had formed incorrectly, and he could be born with defects in his heart, lungs, or more.

Delivery day was hard as Marcela was reminded more than ever how much she missed her mother. It's a daughter's dream to bring home a grandbaby for the woman who had raised her. Despite the pain such thoughts can dredge up, Marcela's sorrow turned to unburdened joy when Lorenzo ended up being born completely healthy.

Life didn't immediately become perfect by any means, and Marcela still had to overcome a struggle with severe postpartum depression, the kind that produced dangerous suicidal tendencies. After six months, by the grace of God, she found complete relief.

Several years later, Marcela had a second son, Leonardo. She hasn't stopped clinging tight to the Rock of Ages, and has devoted herself to exemplifying Christ's love for the downcast and brokenhearted, knowing full well that she was among them at one point. Her goal isn't to hide behind religiosity and pseudo-holiness, but rather to be there for the people who need Him the most.

CHAPTER 3

A "Double Done Deal"

Behold, I am doing a new thing; now it springs forth, do you not perceive it?

I will make a way in the wilderness and rivers in the desert.

ISAIAH 43:19 (ESV)

The Dominican Republic

MANNY AND CARENNY Acosta were born in the Dominican Republic and came from massive families on both sides. When they got married, the first major hurdle they had to overcome was a big one. Would they be having kids? In Dominican culture, children are woven into the very fabric of family identities. Uncles, aunts, cousins. Everyone rallies together to raise the next generation. This kind of "it takes a village" mentality became, unfortunately, kind of alien to many Western cultures as the value of the traditional family deteriorated. It's a different world over here in so many ways, and so when it came to the question of kids, Manny and Carenny weren't just negotiating personal hopes; they were navigating two cultural maps of what having "enough kids" even means. Big families were the name of the game in the DR, but in America where they would really start their married lives, large families are a lot rarer.

To Manny, this was never even a question. Of course! Of course they would have kids! Multiple was a given! He had wanted to be a father since he was young and looked forward to it all his life. To Carenny, this was a much more nuanced conversation. They went back and forth on this issue for years until they eventually ended up in the US and had their first child. The two instantly fell in love with him, and Carenny was glad that they had been afforded the chance to have a son. Manny was ecstatic to find out that the baby would be a boy. He had always wanted his first kid to be a son. *First?* Carenny scoffed every time he brought up the idea of a "first." No, this was the *only* one. This was good. No more kids.

As their son grew, so did Manny's desire for him to have a sibling. He had grown up with siblings, and they were a huge part in shaping the man he became. Manny would regularly ask about expanding the family, but Carenny wouldn't budge. Postpartum depression that lasted for months after the delivery compounded this issue. She was in no mood to experience that again.

Carenny would lie awake at night, heart aching with every baby cry drifting through the walls. She was grateful for the son she'd had, but haunted by the memories of the darkness she'd slipped into postpartum. Each month, she told herself, "Never again," but the conviction with which she said these words began to wane. Each time she saw in Manny's eyes a hopeful gaze, a bit of her own longing sparked within her. It was at three in the morning, when Carenny, half awake, comforted by the warmth of her newborn who clung to her, confessed to herself, *I'm scared I'll break again. But I'm also scared I'll regret not trying.* "Do you want a brother? A sister?" She smiled down at her son. He had finally fallen back asleep. She was no longer as convinced about not having any more kids. *I'm scared I'll regret not trying.* Would that regret not be worse than anything else life could throw at her? To live into old age with that subtle ache of wondering, "What if?" That wondering is a special kind of pain, and any of us young folks who've been around for at least more than fifty years can testify to the fact that regret only deepens with age. It's as your life begins to settle that you have time to focus on all the things that could've been. Carenny could see that question of "What if?" defining her every move in the future. Every school event, play, concert, or graduation that they'd attend for their son. At every milestone, she'd be wondering, "What if?" What if they'd had more than one? What if they'd tried?

It was that night that she realized that true love often means leaning into fear.

Carenny gave Manny an ultimatum as she began to warm up to the idea of having another baby. One day, as Manny was coming home from his job as a construction manager, Carenny wrote out a list of "demands," if you will. He read it and took the challenge. She had written that if he could start earning a certain amount of money by a certain point, then they could consider having another baby. I have to say, I'm a huge fan of this strategy. Clear, practical, and to the point.

Manny went on to double that salary in half the time.

Mysterious Ways

Long before the Acostas would walk forward to our altar, Manny's sister Monika in the DR was already part of the web of prayer that was holding their family together. When Monika finally recommended Grace Church via Excel sheet, she wasn't just helping them find a place to worship. In my mind, it was God knitting two continents together into the fabric of one deeply personal story.

You see, while Carenny was issuing ultimatums and Manny was working hard to meet them, the couple had been searching for churches. On a phone call one day, Manny mentioned this search to his sister, who was instantly inspired. A few hours after speaking to her one lazy Saturday afternoon, Manny's phone lit up with an attachment from Monika.

It was an Excel sheet filled with churches near them, organized into columns depending on the language of their main service and their distance from the couple's home. Manny was astounded. In looking through the rather extensive list, a special annotation caught his eye.

GRACE CHURCH OF NORTH BRUNSWICK****	*look at this one. i like the pastor. he is funny*

I won't lie. It feels pretty good to be referred to as the "funny pastor" on an Excel sheet made by someone from way overseas. Apparently, Monika had been watching our live streams for years from the Dominican Republic and had high hopes for her brother and sister-in-law making Grace Church their home. This was despite the fact that the couple had originally been hoping to find a Spanish-speaking church. That, unfortunately, we are not.

But this wasn't just about geography or technology. I mean, do I find it noteworthy that someone halfway across the world introduced the Acostas to churches right in their own back-yard? Do I find it noteworthy that we now have concrete proof of Grace Church's worldwide appeal? Sure, yes. Half joking with that last bit, but there's a reason I bring this up.

It's a fun anecdote, but in Monika's story, it represents so much more than just the means by which her brother and his wife found a place to worship. It was Monika's way of stepping into her own journey of faith alongside her brother. She, too, had been struggling with infertility back home, and compiling that list for her brother was her own prayer and desperation in action. By mapping out every local church near to her family overseas—English, Spanish, bilingual—she was inadvertently being led by God, mapping the path out of her own wilderness even before she'd set foot in one of our services.

The funny pastor became a hit in the Acosta household. After coming for a few services, they fell in love, and as Carenny got more involved with our women's ministries, she started speaking to my wife about trying for a second. With her encouragement, Carenny decided to go in for an IUD removal.

One afternoon, as the ladies were finishing up their weekly meeting, Carenny explained that she was quite nervous about the whole thing. She had been unsure of having a baby for so long, and now that she felt ready, she was afraid it might not go as smoothly as thought.

"You need to talk to the baby pastor," my wife said.

It was me. She was talking about me.

I met with Carenny and Manny during an altar call that week. I asked them what they were hoping to have, and with zero hesitation Manny responded, "A girl!"

I laughed and told them, "Well in that case, you'll have a girl. It's a done deal. Now, all you have to do is get to work."

Far from Over

They conceived much faster than they expected, but the story was really just beginning. While they were over the moon, they also were scared to tell Monika (Manny's sister), about their pregnancy. She had been trying for a baby for much longer than they had—nearly a year and a half by then. They knew Monika would be happy for them, but it was difficult to not feel like they were rubbing their joy in her face. They saw in the way Monika treated their firstborn, her nephew, that she wanted so desperately to be a mom. Monika and her husband were very well prepared for parenthood too, probably more so than Carenny or Manny. During one of their visits, when Manny eventually revealed that Carenny was expecting, he braced himself. To his immense relief, Monika was overjoyed, but he knew her too well to think that the news hadn't impacted her at all. It was then that Manny decided that Monika would need to appear before the altar at Grace Church just as he and Carenny had done, but that would have to wait for the next time they visited. While all this weighed on Manny, Carenny's own pregnancy brought a few worries of its own.

At one appointment, doctors found evidence of what looked like a heterotopic pregnancy. For those who are unfamiliar, a heterotopic pregnancy is an incredibly rare and high-risk complication where there are essentially two simultaneous pregnancies: one in the uterus (gestational sac) and another outside it (ectopic sac). Treatment options, such as surgery, could jeopardize the survival of the uterine pregnancy. Chances of miscarriage also increase. In some cases, the ectopic sac could rupture, causing life-threatening bleeding.

The Sunday after getting this news, the couple came back before the altar and poured out their hearts to our pastors, elders, and deacons. I remember how Manny's face looked like it had been drained of all its color. I remember how Carenny's hands shook as she explained as best she could while her mind was fraying. "There are two," she choked out. "Two growing inside . . . inside *me*, and I—"

I remember how she kneeled at the altar and gripped its wooden corners.

"God please don't let me lose her," she whispered.

Manny slipped off his shoes, knelt by her side, fingers interlaced around hers, and prayed under his breath. At that moment, our entire pastoral staff felt suspended with them. Every prayer, every whispered "It is done" was now their only lifeline against fear.

People scarcely believe me when I say things like this, but it's the truth. They were prayed over by the pastoral staff, and at their next appointment, all problems simply *disappeared*. Doctors weren't fully sure of what changed, but I have no doubts as to who took care of it.

Months later, while Manny was busy at a job site, Carenny discovered that she was a carrier of a fatal genetic disease. Carenny's world seemed to shrink as the doctor rattled off the odds. She staggered out into the waiting room, chewing on her lower lip in order to keep back the sobs that threatened to break free right there in front of what felt like a million pairs of eyeballs. There couldn't have been more than three women waiting for their appointment. She made her way to her car and sat down, her chest heaving as she pulled out her phone and searched for Manny's number.

If her husband was a carrier as well, the chances of her baby being born with it would skyrocket. This would make the baby surviving more than a couple of years highly unlikely.

After getting off the phone with his wife, Manny called the doctor, livid. "Why would you say all that to her? You could've just asked me to come in and get tested!" He shouted at the doctors, lashing out from a place of intense fear.

"Sir, please. We just wanted to ensure that the baby's mother had all the—" The doctors tried in vain to explain.

"You don't know anything yet! You don't know! There's no way you could—you know what? I'm coming now. Do whatever tests you need to. Today."

Manny scheduled an appointment for that afternoon, hopped in his car, and was at the doctor's in about half an hour. He didn't stop praying under his breath till the second the results came back.

They were in the clear. He wasn't a carrier. Another crisis was averted, and on the bright side, they soon learned they were having a girl.

Two in One

Monika and her husband visited the US, and by extension, Grace Church, pretty regularly before and during Carenny's pregnancy. They were incredibly supportive, but Manny knew that deep down, the lack of children was killing his sister. He saw this in every interaction she had with his son. He saw this in how she retreated into herself when no one was looking.

I saw her crying one week during an altar call. This was way before I had even prayed for Manny and Carenny the first time, before I'd even really gotten to know them. I went up to her and told her that everything would be okay, not knowing who her brother was or what was going on in her life. It was a heartfelt, yet standard and purposefully general message of encouragement. You can never fully know what someone's experiencing standing at the altar. It was a few visits after that first time, once Carenny had already gotten pregnant, that Manny and Carenny took Monika's hand and insisted, "We have to get the baby pastor."

When I prayed for her, I used the phrase "It is done" as I have with so many others. Turns out, this became a bit of an inside joke in their household for a few months after that prayer. It took two whole years for their dream to be realized, but it was. Manny came back to me later, saying, "It was done in Columbia." His sister was pregnant!

They announced it by mailing Manny and Carenny a shirt from the DR. It said, *You're gonna be an uncle!* Carenny, who first opened the gift while home alone, didn't fully register what the shirt said. She figured it was a thoughtful gift for her own pregnancy and texted in her family group chat.

CARENNY

Thx so much for the shirt!!! Love you guys

No response. Carenny picked up the shirt again and looked at it closely. *Uncle?* Then, she looked into the box and saw a second, identical package. That one had her name scrawled in the recipient spot. Tearing the plastic open, she saw a complimentary design. *You're gonna be an aunt? Aunt?*

She called Manny, barely containing her joy. He, now also in a state of complete euphoria, proceeded to patch in Monika and his brother-in-law.

Two done deals for the price of one.

A Unique Methodology

Another shockingly vivid example of how God works in unique ways. It's unreal that one of our few dedicated fans in the Dominican Republic recommending our church to a family who lived right in our own backyard is the reason we can even celebrate this story. However, Excel sheets and live streams are not what brought Manny and Carenny to Grace Church. Those things were just tools used by God to orchestrate His plan. Regular, mundane things often become instruments of that plan, and I'm in awe every single time it all comes together.

Watching Manny and Carenny walk that path—and then Monika behind them—I'm reminded of God's promise throughout His Word. God makes roads in the wilderness and rivers in deserts. One answered prayer becomes a beacon for the next. Each "It is done" we speak doesn't just float into the air and disappear. They stake flags in the road, each one reminding others who watch, and ourselves when we falter, of all the times that we declared: "The world can't, but God can."

Somehow, Monika heard about our church and began following it from hundreds of miles away. She told her brother about it, and their attending a few services changed the trajectory of their lives forever. It's part of the reason they decided to go ahead with expanding their family, and the power of prayer they encountered at Grace Church helped them through many trials. In a beautifully poetic, full-circle moment, the same Monika who once recommended the church to her brother in his time of need later found deliverance there after two years of infertility.

Monika and her husband, Jeam, would go on to write us a letter detailing their experience. It's copied below:

Dear Pastor Joseph,

I hope this letter finds you in good health and spirits. This is Jeam Martinez (Manuel Acosta's brother-in-law) and Monika Acosta (Manuel Acosta's sister) writing.

We wanted to take a moment to express our deepest gratitude for the simplest, yet deepest, strongest and powerful prayer anyone said for us during the two years we had been trying to have kids: "It is done!"

Your heartfelt prayer for us to have children has indeed been answered, and we are overjoyed to share the wonderful news that we are expecting to become parents in May 2024. This miracle is a testament to your faith and the power of the prayers we do to our Lord.

Your prayer became our prayer, and in moments of doubt, my husband and I would look at each other and say: "It is done!"

We believe that our child is not only a gift from God but also a testament to the special impact and guidance you have provided to us through my brother's family's life transformation (Manuel, Carenny y Manuel Jr. Acosta).

As we embark on this new journey of parenthood, we look forward to raising our child with the faith that we preach. We are confident that our family will continue to flourish in the light of God's grace.

Once again, thank you from the depths of our hearts for your prayers. We are blessed to have you in our family members' lives.

May God continue to bless you abundantly in your ministry and may His love shine upon you always.

Looking forward to you meeting our miracle baby

With heartfelt gratitude and love,
Jeam, Monika & our little miracle

CHAPTER 4

Please God, No Surprises

Are not five sparrows sold for two pennies? And not one of them is forgotten before God.

Why, even the hairs of your head are all numbered.

Fear not; you are of more value than many sparrows.

    LUKE 12:6–7 (ESV)

ON A RANDOM afternoon in the summer of 2004, a young Joss was blowing off some steam in his family's detached garage. He picked up a set of dumbbells and sat down on the edge of the bench his stepfather had gotten him for his birthday. *Used piece of—,* he thought to himself as the bench groaned beneath him. He looked around, still seeing red. It was earlier that day that he had discovered his five-foot, four-inch Dominican mother could hit like Ali.

Joss always felt angry, and he felt like everyone was always angry at him. That thought made him even angrier. Teenage angst is a terrible thing, and it is almost always worsened by a healthy serving of domestic confusion. A few years prior, Joss's parents separated for what felt like entirely logical reasons.

There wasn't much he could say that placed either parent at fault, and while he lived with his mother, he had no real quarrels with his extremely hard-working biological father, who had moved down south. Joss's stepfather was nothing but kind to him. He was always there to lend an ear, but Joss rarely wanted to take him up on the offer. He didn't want to talk. He wanted to be angry. He wanted to let his heart freeze over so that even if the world around him never made sense, it wouldn't confuse him. He always felt confused, and he hated that. Confused that he was so angry even though, for what it's worth, he lived a good life with a good family who wanted to be there for him. He didn't get why he wouldn't let them.

Joss allowed himself to lie back on the bench. It made a creaking noise. He let the dumbbells rest on his torso as he looked up at the fossil-gray ceiling of the garage. The weight was almost comforting. He closed his eyes and breathed deeply, internalizing everything about the room around him. Everything about his current situation was uncomfortable, and yet, this was where the world made sense.

He was a skinny kid living in New Brunswick, a town that was still new to him after four years. No one liked him at school, he felt that his family didn't like him at home, and truthfully, he didn't even like himself. In the garage, with the used weight set his stepfather had bought him, he felt like he could channel all this inexplicable hatred into putting some meat on his bones.

He gripped the dumbbells harder, feeling the grooves in the metal imprint onto the skin of his palms. He was sweating profusely. *Weird,* he thought before letting his arms drift away from each other and suspend themselves above the asphalt floor. He checked his form and prepared to push the weight up for his first rep.

Cold. I'm cold.

There was no reason he should feel cold, but something akin to the icy breath of a frost giant had fallen over him. It was 90 degrees out, and Joss was freezing.

Pain.

Where did it hurt?

My chest. My chest. It hurts.

The revelation came to him in waves.

The dumbbells fell from his hand. A tight pain seized his left pec, but it wasn't some muscle strain. A hot flash of searing pain stole his breath as a viselike grip tightened on his heart. Joss, clutching his chest, stumbled to the garage door and collapsed onto the grass outside. His vision tunneled, and the strength seemed to vanish from his limbs. The gentle hum of the overhead lightbulb pitched up into a shrill whine that assaulted his ears along with the thunderous heartbeat that pounded inside his skull. The gray of the concrete floors, the brown-green of the dying grass beyond—it all blurred together into a sickening palette. He was only seventeen. *Am I going to die?*

He called out, trying to force the words.

Mom.

Dad?

Help me.

Every time he tried to speak, he felt his lungs heave with exertion.

Every fight he'd ever had, every argument with his parents played in his mind.

I'm not ready to go.

I mean, no one ever is, but Joss felt like this was especially bad timing for him because if he died today . . . how would he be remembered? Would he just be the rebellious teen who yelled at his mother, or that kid who scowled at everyone he saw in the hallways, or the ingrate who refused to appreciate what he had in life? He realized that he was not at all comfortable with the version of himself he was leaving behind.

On his knees, he gazed at the house, hoping his mother was by the window, washing dishes, and would see him.

She did.

Joss survived the ordeal, and as a result of his "come-to-Jesus" moment, began to turn his life around. His stepfather, whom he now just refers to as "Dad," became a powerful source of inspiration to him. He was a good man with a lot of good things to say once Joss was willing to listen. He pursued finance in college, and while working at a financial education office in Newark, met a hardworking single mother named Franceska.

They started dating, both at this point individually committed to their walks with Christ, but struggling to find their footing as a unit. They loved each other, but argued incessantly. It was around this time, in the winter of 2018 (as their lovers' squabbles had reached their boiling point) that a roommate of Franceska's introduced her to a church. Grace Church. Franceska's old college roommate had been going there for some time, but was planning to relocate to New Mexico.

Intrigued by this church that one of her closest friends spoke so highly of, Franceska encouraged Joss to drive them down to North Brunswick one Sunday instead of to their home church in Dumont. They walked through the front doors and fell in love, taken in by the warmth of the congregation and the openness of its leadership.

One Sunday, they heard it announced that the church would be beginning a new semester of couples' groups. The pastors and couples that Joss and Franceska had gotten to meet spoke highly of the group, crediting it for personal breakthroughs in their lives and marriages. Still unsure of their future together, Joss and Franceska decided to take the plunge and start going. They would later find out that the particular group they went to was intended for married couples only. *Whoops.*

Things worked out, and they ended up getting married in 2019. It was then that Joss decided to attend a men's conference in upstate New York. He wanted to work on himself now that he was a husband to the woman of his dreams and the father of a beautiful daughter. In a way, marrying into Franceska's family was like skipping to stage two of parenting. He'd always wanted a daughter, and now he had gotten the chance to be a father to one while skipping the dirty diapers and sleepless nights. His only hope was that he could be half the father his stepfather was.

Joss often admits that his teenage years were characterized by anger, like many of us who've had practice in the "broken family" department. He remembers his stepfather trying to start conversations in the car after school, only to be met with silence. He remembers his stepfather trying to understand more about his passions, only to get stonewalled. It took time for the two of them to find their footing, but on one arid summer afternoon (just a few months before Joss's cardiac episode), his stepfather found Joss in the backyard trampling through the garden, hot and bothered about something or other, fists clenched and jaws set. His stepfather said he'd gotten something for Joss, something that had helped him a lot when he was younger. It was a weight set and a more-than-gently used bench.

He picked up a dumbbell with one arm and placed the other hand on Joss's shoulder. "Grab the other one, son. I'll show you a thing or two."

Joss normally recoiled when this *stranger* dared to call him son, but that day, he recoiled a little less. The next week, you'd find Joss running drills at dawn, doing push-ups in the grass and sprints on the street, breathing out his rage.

Months later, when Joss collapsed, his heart skipping beats like a busted clock, it was that same man who scooped him into his arms and barreled toward the ER, all the while assuring him that he was safe. That it was all going to be okay.

So when he found himself the father of a child who was now looking to him to be her safety and her anchor, he felt the crushing weight of great expectation upon his shoulders. He longed to be the kind of man who could say things like that and truly mean it. *You're safe. It's all going to be okay.* His life was already so confusing. He could say those things to himself and still not fully believe it. How could he be as sure as Dad was?

Grappling with questions about what it really means to be a man in the modern world, he drove north and attended the conference. While there, he came to realize that he had a deep-seated fear of fatherhood and anxiety about whether or not he would be adequate. As part of the conference, he worked to overcome these obstacles and came back prepared to begin trying for a second child. However, modern medicine told the couple that conceiving again would not be easy. Franceska's journey hit a major bump when she was diagnosed with colitis, an inflammation in her gut that, beyond its daily pain, can throw off the balance of hormones needed to conceive. She was also found with a dermoid cyst on her ovary, which, if left unchecked, could damage her egg supply or twist painfully and require emergency care.

The day of her diagnosis, Fran pressed her forehead to the cool glass of the exam room window, the fluorescent lights buzzing overhead. The words *colitis* and *dermoid cyst* still echoed in her brain. *Broken,* she thought. *I'm broken.*

Broken, but not just physically. Her identity as a healthy woman felt shattered. When the nurse left, Fran closed her eyes and wept, not only for the pain she felt in her gut, but for the life she would now never be able to give.

Professionals told the couple that having a second child wasn't impossible, but it was looking increasingly unlikely. Faced with the prospect of never being able to have another baby, Franceska agreed that they needed to act immediately to try and conceive. They had planned to advance their careers to a certain point, make a certain amount of money, and buy a house with certain specifications before they considered more kids. God, however, had different plans.

Months of trying went by to no avail. It was around the fourth month that they approached me for the first time.

I prayed for them, promising that what they were hoping for was a done deal. Then, the months just continued to tick by . . .

FRANCESKA

This morning should've been a dream. I rose from my bed, swung open our cabin window, and breathed the alpine air. *Mmm. Cool moss and pine.* I heard the women's laughter drift across the water. Their happiness was like salt in my open wound.

I am probably, technically, medically infertile. It sickens me to even think about this, but it's the truth. It has been almost fourteen months of trying. The Apollo 11 mission took four days, and those guys literally went to space! Four days to travel to the moon and back. Meanwhile, it's taken us fourteen months to have a baby.

Fourteen months to have a baby.

Fourteen months of waking before dawn to test, blinking blearily at the single line and feeling my stomach knot when it refused to multiply.

Fourteen months of tracing circles in red marker on the fridge door calendar, each *X* for another failure.

Fourteen months of following a schedule, our bodies agreeing to a plan our hearts were losing faith in.

Fourteen months of Joss sliding coffee across the kitchen table at midnight, whispering, "Next month." *Next month. Ha.* As if sheer will could rewrite our biology.

Never did I think that this road was going to be easy. I know there's a fair share of things wrong with me. It's just that when

Pastor Joe first prayed for us, we all felt so sure. He was so confident that we were going to have a baby that I guess I let that confidence rub off on me. With every passing week, I think, *This is it!* And every week, I am disappointed. I've been tossing the pregnancy tests in the trash before Joss gets a chance to ask, but at this point, he usually doesn't.

I'm just so tired, and not in a normal way. Tired in a way that keeps me from wanting to do anything. None of my hobbies interest me anymore. Simply walking through the office or driving Maria to school leaves me feeling winded. I'm fatigued beyond belief. I never really understood when people said, "My heart is heavy" as a way to talk about grief, but I get it now. Sadness has a way of weighing you down.

The rest of the women are down by the lake, unwinding after a long day of sessions. The sun has just started to disappear behind the trees, basking the whole resort in a golden glow as rays of sunlight filter through the leaves. The weather is immaculate, the birds are singing, the squirrels are at play . . . it's a good day.

The rest of the women came on this retreat to spend time in God's presence and soak in the beauty of the Pennsylvania mountainside, all while having fun with some of their closest friends. I thought that's why I came too, but instead of laughing and talking with the others by the lake, I'm letting myself rot in my own misery with the lights out and windows drawn. I'm just too tired.

The door opens, and my roommate, Laura, walks in.

"Fran? Aren't you coming out with us? They've been asking for you by the lake."

I shake my head no, refusing to make eye contact.

"It's a beautiful day outside."

"I know." I say, staring at the corner of my bed.

"Fran, come on. Let's go do something! I feel bad. I've barely seen you all weekend, and we *room* together. Are you doing okay?" Laura takes a seat next to me. I can feel her gaze burning a hole in the back of my head. I stay silent for a time until a weak *no* escapes my lips. It's done. I've committed. Now we're going all the way.

"No. I'm not. Not even close." I turn to face Laura, whose eyes are filled with compassion. "Every week, I stand at the front of the church and help others get prayed for. Every week, I have to put on a face that reminds them to believe. Every week I've got to look strong—no, *be* strong for the people who feel broken and come to church looking for God as if He and I are best friends. But right now, I don't know where He is."

"Fran . . ."

"Last Sunday, a young mom was crying at the altar. She confided in me, Laura. Told me her marriage was falling apart. I gave her a hug. I told her everything was going to be okay. I quoted the Bible to her. I did it all correctly." I look down at my hands. *I did it all correctly. Like I was an actor who was nailing her dialogue.*

"You did . . ."

"But what are we really doing here, huh? At some point, we're all just cosplaying therapists. Everything I spit out at the altar is just following some script!"

"Fran, you don't really believe that—"

"I don't know what I believe." I realize I cut her off, but I can't really be bothered to care. "I don't know what I'm telling the people that come up there every Sunday. I don't know why I decided to put myself in the position to watch others come up and receive their comfort, their victories, week after week, only to be the person left holding the box of tissues. God makes me watch Him do things for others."

I'm glaring at Laura now, as if she were somehow responsible for my mess. As if she could answer me on God's behalf.

"Fran, don't ever feel like God doesn't see the heart you have for the people who need Him. What you're going through—"

"I know He sees it. He sees everything. He sees me sitting in here rotting instead of having a good time with my friends, and yet—and yet—" I feel Laura wrap me in a hug, and the tears just start to flow. "I'm just—I'm just so tired."

"I know."

"I'm so tired, Laura. I can't move. I can't think."

"I understand."

I love that she isn't saying too much.

"I'm not doing the best health-wise. I honestly don't know how I plan to bring another healthy human life into this world when I feel like I'm just . . . melting!"

"Melting?"

"Melting. Melting into a puddle and going down a storm drain. And through all this, God is where?"

Laura lets me cry for a while before speaking again. It takes a special person to understand that sometimes, words are poor comfort, and other times, a kind word can make all the difference in the world. "If it's strength you need, you'll have it."

I pick my head up.

"I know the pain of what it's like to see what you see, do what you do every week, and still be waiting on God to show up for you. Honestly, I'm waiting on God for a pretty big win right now. It's been a rough few months for the family."

"What?" I ask. "How?" Her face exuded a kind of contentment that I could only dream of. "What's going on?"

"Not important right now. What I want you to know is that there's no chance He's forgotten about you or your baby. Who *is* coming, by the way. It's impossible for Him to forget, He knows everything that's gonna happen. Time is like nothing to him. So in His eyes, maybe your kid's already here!"

Super trippy.

"Trippy, I know. But I heard a pastor mention it once, and I've always wanted to use it myself." That manages to force a small laugh out of the both of us. It feels good to laugh. "I know it's been, what? Fourteen, fifteen months? I'm sure the only thing you can think about right now is . . . well, if having a baby is impossible at this point. Am I right?"

"It is. At least clinically."

"But you and I both know that God hates that word. *Impossible.* Impossible doesn't exist for him. But if I'm being honest, I don't know when He plans to make good on this."

"I guess that's what makes it *His* plan."

"Right! But what I do know with all my heart is that if it's strength you need right now, He'll give it to you. If it's comfort, you'll have that too. And I *know* you're gonna have that baby in your hands. I know everybody is saying this, but it's always just a matter of time till He comes through. I know this for a fact because in my life, I've walked through fire, but I haven't ever been burned. I've felt like I'm sinking, but He's never let me drown."

"That's . . . that's . . ."

"Pretty good, huh?" Laura says, smiling. "I know, I'm thinking it too. I've been on kind of a roll today."

We laugh again. I didn't know it would feel this good to laugh.

She continues, "I mean, we believe in a virgin birth. Crazier things have happened, right?"

I feel myself beaming. To make light of what was crushing my mind all these months is honestly freeing. It feels like I'm rolling my eyes at the bogeyman.

JOSS

Sometimes, like right now, I catch myself thinking about the day that I almost died. I stepped out of the office for what was supposed to be "ten minutes of fresh air," and it's been one hour. I've walked several city blocks while lost in thought, and somehow, a cup of coffee has mysteriously appeared in my hand during that intense think tank with myself.

I turn a corner and am immediately greeted by a new, alarmingly diverse palette of smells. Some are nice, like the scent of fresh shawarma from the halal cart down the street, and some are just . . . interesting. It's a city. What're you gonna do?

I make my way over to a nearby bench, sit down, and finally take a sip of my coffee. It is now a disgusting lukewarm. I realize I'm sitting right by an outdoor basketball court, the ones on the corner of city blocks bordered by chain-link fences. Like most of these courts I've ever been on, this one looks worn and in desperate need of some TLC. The painted lines on the court are just barely visible, and the hoop doesn't even have a net around it.

To one side, a group of middle-aged men wearing tank tops and oversized basketball shorts are playing a pickup game while blasting Public Enemy. This confirms for me that they are at least my age or older. Those guys are good, but pretty old-school. At the other end of the court is a far more interesting game.

A young father (he can't be older than thirty) is standing between his roughly eight-year-old-son and the hoop that seemed to taunt the little boy with its height. The dad's tall, easily over six feet. I see him encourage his son, who, gathering his strength, makes a push forward. The father makes a big show of trying to defend the little guy before feigning a huge fall, allowing the kid to shoot. He misses, but immediately gets under the net to catch the rebound and try again.

"Why don't we try playing on the same team this time, kid?" I hear the dad say, smiling as he picks himself up off the ground.

"No! I'm gonna make the next one." The kid's face hardens in determination.

"You sure, big guy?" the dad teases.

"I know I can. Just you try and guard me." The kid starts dribbling again, preparing to make another attempt.

Sometimes, in moments like these, I remember my father. Correction, *fathers*. I know some stepchildren do not maintain the best relationship with their biological dads, but that wasn't the case for me. The day I almost died, I remember regretting so much. The thing I regretted the most was how I had treated the people around me, specifically my parents. Divorce is an ugly thing, and it can turn kids into ugly people. I never realized how fortunate I was that the divorce my parents went through was simply out of sheer incompatibility, and not for more serious reasons. On top of that, the man my mother decided to marry is one of the greatest men I've had the pleasure of knowing. I didn't realize how lucky I was because teenage angst is a powerful drug.

I hated everything, but on that day I promised myself I would start living like I was happy to be alive. The first person I remember seeing as I drifted in and out of consciousness was my stepdad.

From that day onward, my stepdad and I began to cultivate a real relationship. We bonded over our mutual love of baseball, action movies, and groups that my kids would one day roll their eyes at and call "dad rap," like Public Enemy. I could confide in him about anything and everything. The kids at school, girls, my plans for the future, how to get jacked—we talked about it all. He was, and still is, my best friend. I put him on a pedestal growing up, and I still hope to be even just a fraction of the man he was. When I moved out and became part of my own blended family, I saw that life tends to come full circle. I can't tell you how great it feels to step up to the role of fatherhood like someone once did for me. I don't think he can ever understand how much his presence in my life meant, and I just hope I can be there in the same way for my Maria.

But I didn't completely cut off my biological father. I look up to him in a completely different way. He was a first-generation immigrant and worked several jobs daily just to put bread on the table. I'll always respect that, but as a result of the lifestyle he had to live, he was never around. I still keep in contact with him, and remembering how he worked himself to the bone for our family is often the reason I get up in the morning or feel a pang of guilt when I let myself slack off.

When my mom first married my stepdad, I was bitter because I had just experienced a father who couldn't be present. Then I was given a father who could, and I didn't want him to be. It took almost dying to get over that little hiccup.

My dads are my heroes, but I'm no hero. I spent a weekend with some of my church brothers at a conference, and there I had to come to grips with the fact that I have a deep-seated fear of fatherhood. Kind of an inconvenient thing to find out as a father. It's not that I didn't want children. No, Maria's my whole life, and all I've been thinking about lately is the baby that's on the way. The reality is that I've spent my whole life idolizing two male figures. One of a provider who would go to any lengths to make sure his family was comfortable, and one of a close source of emotional support who made the time to be present for me in spite of all my flaws. I fear I can't be both perfectly without sacrificing one way or the other. These great men stand behind me and cast a shadow over all that I accomplish. It's been a slow process understanding that and dismantling the fear that I won't measure up.

The only one who can do it all perfectly, without faltering in any area, is God Himself. He's the kind of father I should really be looking to as a guide. I've known Him as a provider, a comforter, a father, and a friend. It's a process trying to be all of these at the same time when you're not Him. On top of all that, I've been trying to be a better son to my mother. Not that we've ever had serious problems, but now that I'm a parent, I've got a new appreciation for what mothers do to keep the household sane.

I also fear that things might be different with a baby of my own. I've always wanted to have one, but now that it's pretty much a done deal, I'm not really sure how to do the whole "new dad" thing. I can only hope Fran and the newborn will be patient with me.

Patience. Fran and Maria have been so patient, it hurts. I ended up buying Maria a puppy (Chewy) two weeks ago because the new sibling we've been talking about is taking its sweet time. The girl hasn't given up hope. I know Fran hasn't been feeling the best, but she took a trip with some of the women from the church. Hopefully, the mountain air will be good for her, and if it isn't enough, I've got another trip lined up for her when she gets back.

Okay, fine. It's a work trip. She and I both have to go. But is a work trip really a work trip if it's in Atlantic City?

We made the drive up the shore at sunset, windows down. Fran was napping in the passenger seat while I tapped along to an old Sinatra CD (not usually my vibe, but it felt appropriate for a trip to a casino town).

After getting settled in our hotel, we splurged on a diner dinner, downing Tower-of-Babel-level stacks of pancakes and coffee. While she nursed her cup, I saw Fran nervously twisting the hem of her sweater.

We couldn't afford to be out too late, as our first day of seminars would start early next morning, but we found the time for a quick visit to the Boardwalk. Under the flashing lights, Fran stopped and asked me, "Do you ever feel like we're rolling the dice on this thing?"

I shrugged and slid my hand into hers. It was strangely quiet. No fortune-tellers or hokey gimmicks. Just us, standing in the salt air, reminding ourselves that hope was as real as the waves slapping against the wooden posts beneath. We found an ice cream spot that was somehow still open and shared a vanilla sundae. One order, two spoons. For the first time in months, we laughed, and our laughter wasn't edged with anxiety.

It was already later than I'd expected it to be. We'd be dead tired for our first seminar in the morning, but if there was ever a place to make a gamble . . .

FRANCESKA

Never in my life did I think I'd say this, but I guess magic happens in Atlantic city. Oh, Monopoly City! Las Vegas of the East Coast! How I love your saltwater taffy, your stretches of marshland and armies of reeds. Your bright-colored carpets and brighter lighting displays that all seem to point the way to being completely miserable. To think, God can work even in a crazy town like that!

Little Catalina was conceived about eight months ago when Joss and I took a trip to the "World's Playground" for a financial advisors' convention. How endless seminars about customer satisfaction and the growing influence of AI in the consulting world could ever lead to that is beyond me.

God can't want it more than you want it for yourself. This is something I've been forced to learn through the wait. I can look back now and pretend like I knew this all along, but you all know that's not the truth. I can repeat that little one-liner to others who are waiting on their promises like I'm a wise old soul who just happened to know that.

I'm fully kidding. I can't overstate how powerful the testimonies of others who went through what I did were for me. Their words of encouragement kept me from growing to hate the God I know I love. I had to hold firm to the idea that what He's promised, He will ultimately do. If I stop wanting it just because He's taking his time, then what purpose will the wait up to that point have served? We're taught to run the race with endurance, to fight the good fight. What do these things have in common? They require patience, setting your mind on a goal beyond the present situation, and worst of all, cardio.

Granted, not every prayer is going to be answered with a yes. Sometimes it's a no, sometimes it's a yes, and sometimes it's, "In a little, kiddo." But our job through all that is to hold fast, especially if it's that third option. Like kids, if we're told to hang on for a little, we decide that we no longer want what we asked for. That's got to make you wonder if what you wanted was really that important to you to begin with. If we stopped hoping for what we've been promised, it would mean that all the tears we've shed (not one of which He doesn't notice), and the faith we've demonstrated up until that point would be for nothing.

I'm counting the seconds till Catalina arrives . . .

JOSS

I don't like surprises. Never have. My wife threw me a surprise birthday party when we first got married. It's not that I didn't appreciate the effort, but let's just say that we spoke, and she never has again.

I especially didn't want surprises that had anything to do with Catalina. We asked to know Catalina's gender almost immediately. No surprises. I like to know what clothes to get and all that.

We also knew she was going to look like me thanks to 3D imaging tech (science can be so cool sometimes). I remember Fran turned to me when we got our first look and said, "She's got your nose."

We wanted no surprises around the time of labor. Those were especially big surprises, so we agreed that Fran would be induced. Finally, the day has come.

We left our house around four, stopped for food at a Dominican spot we like on the way (zero waiting in line because God had our backs), got through the check-in process at record speeds, and now I'm waiting with my mother in an empty hospital corridor.

I know for a fact that I want to be present (and alert) when Catalina's born, so it's probably a good idea that I get some shut-eye while I can. The doctors warned me that it could be a long while before I can go in and see Fran for the actual birth. I'm stressed, and nervous beyond belief, but my wife says I'm the type to sleep through anything, so I might as well put that skill to good use.

I pull my baseball cap down and let my chin rest on my upper chest, partially burying my face in the collars of my wool button-down. I ask my mom to wake me when it's time and let myself drift into a deep sleep. *Please God, no surprises.*

"Joss? Wake up. Wake up, son." My mother's voice becomes clear as I awake. Her soft, warm whisper is hardly a wake-up call, but her ice-cold fingers definitely did the trick.

"Mom? It's time?" I mumble as I straighten up.

"No."

I look at my mother, and see concern written across her face.

"I'm waking you because it should've been time a while ago."

Oh, no. Surprises.

FRANCESKA

Giving birth is beautiful, but sometimes the process can feel like a war of attrition, and sometimes straight-up war. This whole thing can feel like it's designed to slowly wear away at you. That may be true for a lot of things in this life, but it feels a hundred times more intense when you know that another living being is depending on you to fight through everything that gets thrown your way. So you know . . . no pressure. While my baby depends on her mother, her mother is depending completely on God.

Forty minutes! The epidural guy spent forty minutes stabbing me with his needle trying to make it work. Forty whole minutes of literal war.

I'm being a little hard on him. After all, I understand a herniated disk doesn't make for easy administering of the epidural. The poor man was probably trying his best, but that doesn't change the fact that we are now hilariously behind schedule. That epidural fiasco was about a half hour ago, and now I'm sitting here waiting to try again.

This room, though I haven't been in it very long, is starting to make me sick. The honeydew green of the walls, the gentle murmur of the birth team as they prepare, and the choir of delivery room equipment gently chirping and humming in the background has only grown to irritate me. It's the nerves. I can feel it. I'm also starting to feel contractions.

Knock, knock. And so the warfare continues.

The anesthesiologist has made two attempts, and is now preparing for a third.

This room has a way of disorienting you. I've been sitting hunched over on the edge of this hospital bed, staring at the slate gray of the tile floor far too long for my liking. Earlier, I tried to have a conversation about why this whole thing was proving to be so difficult. The doctors said some words to me, but I can't recall a single one of them right now.

Ah! I inhale sharply as I feel the icy finger of the needle make contact with my back once again. I pray, hoping this is—

God! I exclaim, as an intense burst of what felt like electricity shoots down my spine and through my legs. I close my eyes almost instinctively, and when I open them, I find myself staring at my left leg, now suspended parallel over the floor. In a swift, blink-and-you-miss-it motion, my leg had shot up and was now frozen in midair. *Stay calm. Breathe.* I can't see the doctor, but I wouldn't be surprised if he was sweating through his white coat right about now.

Okay, it's coming down. I feel him slowly remove that finger of death from my spine, and some semblance of sensation returns to my leg.

The fourth attempt worked, so that's one battle won. I'm trying to focus, trying to keep my mind on what is about to happen, but my stream of consciousness is polluted with the stench of this one, ugly word. *Paralysis.*

It's hard to breathe as I wonder if, after all this time, bringing Catalina into this world could cost me so severely. I'm not entirely sure what happened, but since the "exorcist" incident (which I will probably have nightmares about for a while), I haven't really been able to feel my legs. The fourth epidural did what it was supposed to, but as the nurses wheeled me back to this room, I told them that it felt like I was "half a person."

What I was *trying* to articulate is that I couldn't feel my legs.

Cold! It's cold! A wet *squelch* accompanied by the kiss of soaked fabric on my shin alerts me to what had been happening in the delivery room while I was zoned out.

"How are we feeling, Fran?" the nurse said, looking up at me from the edge of the bed where she was holding a wet towel against my right leg. The feeling of water trickling down my calves and onto the bedsheet below is uncomfortable, sure, but I feel nothing short of elation. I can feel it! I can feel that towel on my right leg!

I nod to the nurse. She smiles back and moves the towel to the left leg. I mentally brace myself, preparing to feel that initial cold bite of the wet towel when . . .

Nothing. You can't be serious. I see the nurse's mouth move, but the words are a muddled mess to my ears. *Nothing?*

She moves the towel, and as she approaches my upper thigh, I start to feel again. I nod at her, shaking welled-up tears loose from my eyes.

Paralysis.

I'm in no position to dwell on it too much. I might've won that battle with the epidural, but it left me with a nasty scar to remember it by. I see them bring in Joss and explain to him what he needs to know before we go on with the actual birth. I have to fight to repress the doubts and fears that feel like animals clawing at the bars of my mind, fighting to get loose.

We get to know God pretty well through our walk in this life, but sometimes we can forget that there's another side to the world we can't see, and that side is run by a guy who loves nothing more than to steal, kill, and destroy the goodness we're meant to experience. The battle is really just ensuring that he doesn't get to do any of that. And he won't.

Joss takes my hand. *Three pushes and she's out.* Words from a casual conversation with Pastor Alicia many months ago flash into my head. She seemed so sure of it. The same way Pastor Joe had been sure of this baby's arrival.

Three pushes and she's out . . .

JOSS

Three pushes and she was out. Catalina was born, and our world made sense again. That's one thing my wife said late that night that I'll never forget. *Everything makes sense again.* I couldn't agree more. When I look into Catalina's cinnamon-brown eyes, at her little face that so resembles mine, it all makes sense. I also told Fran that we should enjoy this feeling for all it's worth, because once little Catalina starts walking and (especially) talking, things'll go back to being all upside down. That's part of what makes being a dad so rewarding. It never gets dull. You've gotta keep that outlook on it; otherwise, the teenage years will kill you.

Sitting in church this morning with my wife and now *two* beautiful daughters feels like a fantasy. There are a lot of things I was excited for as the dad of a newborn for the first time, but one of those things was without a doubt her first church visit. I can promise you one thing, Catalina: You won't have to wait as long as I did to know that you have a Father above who loves you more than I ever could.

I can tell Catalina is going to grow up to love music and

worship. I was watching her the entire time, mouth agape, fully engrossed in the art of live praise. *Just like her father.*

I watch Pastor Courtney step up to the microphone for announcements.

"Next semester's couples' group kicks off in just a few weeks," he begins, scanning the room. "Now, all *married* couples are welcome to join the group you see behind me. All *married* couples. If you're still waitin' on that ring, don't fret. There are plenty of other groups just right for you. But this one here," he gestures to the projector screen, "is for married couples only."

My chest tightens, and I glance at Fran. Her eyes are bright with recognition. We'd poured our hopes into that room long before we ever said, "I do." Pastor Courtney gives us a sidelong glance and shrugs his shoulders, a half grin tugging at his lips. Then, he moves on to the next announcement.

I turn to Fran and see she's already looking at me. And we smile.

Conclusion
Invested

Fran and Joss were quick to get involved at Grace Church. This is a trait I always love to see, as it brings me back to my early years as a Christian. I was young and brimming with an intense passion to do whatever I could in God's house. They joined our ushers and greeters team, which was responsible for welcoming people at the door, helping guests feel comfortable, coordinating seating, and assisting with prayer at the altar. A large part of this job was, as Fran spoke about earlier, comforting those who are grieving. Church is a beautiful place where tears flow freely, regardless of social background. I've watched teenagers and fully grown adults alike bawl at the altar like little children, and I'm no different. There is something deeply moving about the power of God, and being a good usher means supporting people as they lay it all out there before Him.

They asked me to pray over them one Sunday after hearing a sermon in which I touched upon other couples that had experienced miraculous conceptions here at Grace Church. Fran and Joss decided that they would bring their fears to the altar, just as they had helped so many others do.

Every Sunday for over a year, I stood at the altar, watching Fran and Joss make their way up to the front weekly, and every time, my chest tightened. It wasn't because I doubted God's timing, but because I knew how crushing that empty cradle space must feel. While preaching, I'd find myself thinking, *What do I say to them today?* My sermon notes blurred as I pictured Fran's quiet tears masked by her smile, Joss's broken heart masked by his warmth. I prayed in silence as I preached, wrestling with my own impatience. *God, please. You've brought them this far . . .*

This is where some of my human fallibility becomes super obvious. I'm operating under the guidance of the supernatural, and yet my human intelligence told me that I should be worried for some reason. *What if they don't conceive?*

This idea sprouts up in my mind like a weed every now and then. I feared that them being new members placed a greater weight on this miracle. Would them not conceiving reflect poorly on me? Or the church? Or God?

You might find this silly, but understand that I get deeply invested in every couple I pray for. I regularly would make eye contact with Fran when I was delivering sermons that touched on miracles, faith, or anything in that vein. We would silently exchange glances that spoke a thousand words. I looked at her with an expression that seemed to ask, "Anything?" She would respond with an expression of her own that said, "Not yet."

Their story was one of the first times I really clocked my own investment, and how deep it ran. Once I'd noticed it, it became easy to pinpoint how it had popped in the stories of others without my even knowing.

I remember one morning in my office, the sunlight cutting through drawn blinds, I caught myself rehearsing the words I'd use if Fran and Joss told me it was all too much. My heart was parallel to theirs. I was waiting, hoping, and fearing just as they were. It was then that I realized that in all the stories you're reading about, I'm more than just a pastor. In these families' lives, I'm a fellow traveler in the ache of unanswered prayer.

They were new to the church. Would the confidence that I'd put behind that prayer mean nothing if they never had that baby?

Even I often need a reminder that the ultimate outcome isn't really in my hands. The One who enables me to pray for people and who makes miracles possible doesn't operate on my schedule. I think how invested I get is a double-sided issue. It's what makes these stories that much more special, but it also creates quite an emotional roller coaster for me as I wait with the couple.

I Prayed for You

After many months and a lot of tears from everyone involved, when I finally got the news that Fran was pregnant, I could hardly contain my own joy (and relief). The way they broke the news was especially sweet.

They bought a book with a cover that read:

I PRAYED FOR YOU

The inscription was accompanied by a beautiful illustration of a big momma bear holding up her cub. Inside, they left me a little note. The idea is that once Catalina gets a little older, I'll give her that book with a note of my own inside so that she'll never forget what a miracle she was.

To this day, I can sense Catalina watching me as I preach on Sundays and smiling at me during worship. It's almost like she already knows.

CHAPTER 5

The Philosophy of Joy

Weeping may tarry for the night, but joy comes with the morning.
PSALM 30:5 (ESV)

Around the World

JOY'S PHILOSOPHY HAS always been that "family makes the world go round." She credits her upbringing in a tight-knit, traditional community for this, seeing as strong family ties were the cornerstone upon which their lives were built. She was taught that family was everything. Family made life meaningful.

"We won't always be around," she says. "We must think about how we will pass on the torch, the collective knowledge we have accumulated, and to whom this will all be passed on."

All through Joy's life, she knew that, above all, she would be a loving mother to children of her own one day. Little did she expect such a simple, human desire to come attached with years of confusion and strife. Before we can get to any of that, however, we must first track the worldwide journey that led her to where she is now. Ready? Here we go.

She was born in Baltimore and moved to Nigeria when she was four. She spent about twelve years there before moving to London after finishing grade school to be with her mother (who had long since separated from her father who was still living in Nigeria). Her time with her birth parents proved difficult, with marital tension leading to an unstable home environment. She was torn between her mother and father during separation. She grew up wishing desperately to experience what it was like to grow up in a "normal" household. She was granted this wish when she moved back to Baltimore to live with her god-father and godmother (her older brother's former first-grade teacher). That older brother ended up in Norway.

Each uprooting taught Joy that "home" was less of a place and more the people who stayed by her side. In Nigeria, a place where aunts, uncles, and cousins form a safety net, she saw how children thrived in a community that celebrated them to the fullest. She managed to pull that goodness out of her time in that country, even while her own familial dynamic was turbulent at best. In London, surrounded by hustling pro-fessionals, she longed for the same warmth even while the bustle of the city kept her life plenty busy. Relational turbulence never ceased to be a factor in her worldview, even with her birth parents now miles apart. Coming back to Baltimore, she carried the developmental scars and blessings of the many lives she'd lived.

Finding an answered prayer in her two loving godparents, Joy's hopes of one day raising a nuclear family of her own were renewed. Joy completed her undergraduate studies at the University of Maryland and then went Ivy League for her master's degree at the Wharton School of the University of Pennsylvania. It was in her final two years at Wharton that she met her husband, a friend's older brother, while they were having lunch.

The two of them clicked almost instantly, and while her friend cooked, Joy decided that this was the man she wanted to spend the rest of her life with. Neither of them was interested in a casual fling. They were looking for a serious relationship, and seeing as they aligned on that, they started dating. Three years later, they were engaged. Another two years later, in 2010, they got married in their home country of Nigeria.

As most people with in-laws can guess, parents on both sides were eager to see grandkids. Joy and her husband, however, took their time getting settled in as a couple before even thinking about bringing children into the equation. They gave birth to their first baby late in 2012, and two years later, after they had a handle on the whole "first-time parent" deal, they started trying for a second. This is where things got complicated.

Two years went by. At this point, around 2016, Joy could be considered infertile. Back in Nigeria, in Joy's first community, pregnancies were celebrated like harvest festivals. For better or for worse, a woman's place in the community often hinged on her children. To go childless for years carried with it the weight of shame you didn't feel you could really talk to anybody about. This was a reality that Joy never expected would weigh so heavily on her own heart.

What went wrong? Everything was smooth the first time around. As the couple began to approach their third year with no luck, Joy began to wonder if they should start looking into medical intervention. In particular, she was hoping her husband would come around on getting himself tested to make sure that everything was exactly as it should be. However, as she put it, getting men to agree to things like that can sometimes feel like "pulling teeth."

God's House

Joy always wanted to be in a church environment conducive to children. Growing up, her faith was everything to her, and she needed her children to have that same experience. Joy's first child, Ore Dola (whose name means "friendship turned to wealth"), regularly attended church with her. However, the New Jersey "super-megachurch" she was attending just didn't feel right. Perhaps it was simply too big to feel the sense of community she was used to and wanted to pass on to her child. Through prayer, Joy asked the Lord for direction and stumbled upon Grace Church.

Her first Sunday at Grace Church, you could almost see the relief wash over her. If it was a community for her kids she'd been looking for, she'd found it here.

She paused at the entrance of one of the children's church classrooms and let out a soft, contented sigh. The room was painted in warm, inviting colors like sunshine yellow and sky blue. Low tables were arranged on technicolor, stage-sized rugs. About a dozen children were clustered there, wide-eyed and singing worship songs at the top of their lungs, their little arms reaching for the sky. Joy stepped back and looked down the hallway to see a volunteer helping the second graders hang up drawings on a bulletin board already displaying the Jonah pictures of the fourth graders and the "my favorite verse" projects of the third graders. At the end of the hallway were double doors leading into a larger hall where the laughter of middle schoolers resounded.

Joy saw her daughter standing off to the side, fiddling with the hem of her shirt. A teacher, spotting her hesitation, invited Joy to join her daughter in the classroom.

"Let's draw with Mommy, love." The teacher took Ore Dola's hand and guided her over to a table filled with other children who were busy coloring. "It'd be huge for her to have you with her for just a few minutes. It helps them get more comfortable. Here, try this."

"Oh, of course. Yes." Joy knelt down and offered Ore Dola the brightly colored crayon the leader had placed in her hands.

"Can anyone tell Ms. Joy what we are learning about today?" the teacher asked the class, beaming as almost every hand shot up almost instantly with competing cries of "Me! Me! Me!"

"Noah!" shouted the kid who'd been called on. He bounced up in front of Joy and Ore Dola to tell her his rendition of the story. Joy clapped appreciatively when he finished grandly with, "And then the rainbow came!"

This was more than just childcare. This was teaching worship to little hearts.

She helped her daughter begin tracing out the outline of the ark, but before long, Ore Dola was engrossed in conversation with the peers around her. Joy, taking her cue, slowly got up to leave. It was that moment that made her choice of church clear to her. As she stood by the entrance, preparing to leave, she smiled as her daughter's eyes continued to flick back to her in delighted surprise.

It's like I always say. Grace Church is a "church for children."

I've always thought that you could tell a lot about a person from their name. This isn't foolproof science or anything, just gut instinct. One thing I can say for sure is that you'd be hard-pressed to find someone who embodies "joy" like Joy does. She doesn't just smile. Her grin practically lights up the room, and you can see people soften when she's around. In worship, I'll catch her singing, eyes lifted as if God was watching right above where she was standing. I've seen her put a newcomer next to her at ease more than once. I can always spot her in the congregation as I preach, especially when I'm preaching on the tougher stuff. I glance down and there she is, eyes bright and nodding at me.

But for all that sunshine, a few of us, like my wife, knew that her life was no picnic. After years of wrestling with unanswered prayers for a child, Joy poured her heart into helping her brother through a brutal season of addiction in Norway. It was this that showed me that this "joy" was far from naivete. When someone in her family was threatened by the monster of addiction, one that was all too familiar for me, she didn't stand by and wait for someone to come to her brother's rescue. She made a decision, booked a flight, and was in Norway within days of her brother's worsening condition coming to her attention. This trip came with weeks of late-night drives through unfamiliar streets and difficult conversations in hospital lobbies. She came home scarred, but unbroken. It seemed like her trust had been somehow strengthened by the darkness she and God had faced together. When she walked back into Grace Church after her return, she confided in me about her next big hope.

It was an altar call where I said, "Listen, if there's any anointing I've got, it's the baby anointing. If you're having trouble conceiving, come on up here."

Joy was sitting with her mother, who was visiting from the UK. Her mother, naturally, prompts her. Little did she know that Joy had already planned to come up. She made her way forward and explained her situation to me. At first, I was a little taken aback. This woman who I recognized for being one of the most vibrant in a sea of faces every week was now in front of me saying that she had been struggling to have children for *years*. She had been trying for five years and was now approaching the sixth. I was shocked at how she was holding up, broken internally, yet standing before me with faith. I assured her, in that same faith, that it was done. She would conceive.

Six years can feel like both a blink and an eternity. January after January, Joy would make a hopeful New Year's prayer. She was fully convinced that each first of January brought with it an opportunity for her second to be born. She began picturing what her child's birthday would be like. She began thinking about his or her name. How it would look when written out on a birth certificate or a private school application or a rec soccer registration form.

Joy would pace the church parking lot before service, as if a miracle would meet her right there in the lot unannounced. Come fall, she'd watch leaves drift by her window as she sat at the kitchen table with her husband, both of them holding a test in shaking hands. In the winter, decorations went up one day and seemed to come down the next.

Joy dominated in the boardroom and excelled at every professional endeavor she put her hand to. She was the pride of her manager, and beloved by some coworkers (and the envy of others). Yet, no level of corporate excellence could console her broken heart. No fiscal quarter projection could forecast the depth of the pain she'd felt with every passing month. She'd navigated so much pressure with poise, but the unpredictability of infertility wasn't something her MBA had prepared her for.

She got promotions at work, got new furniture, got rid of old furniture, met new people, lost contact with some old friends, attended weddings and bridal showers, and through it all, that ache stuck around. She took up journaling on Wednesdays and dodged parenting blogs through the week. Her algorithm had decided to taunt her:

What to expect when you're expecting!
Five things soon-to-be-mommies need!
Baby transitioning to solids? Everything you need to know.
What should you do before baby #2 arrives? Read now!

There was a time when she'd excitedly read and saved these articles, but by the time she came to see me, her hope reserves had been running on near empty for a while. Near empty, but not entirely. She came to that altar in faith, and she walked away with the hope infusion she needed to carry her for a few months more.

She went home revitalized by the faith she had seen me speak with. Faith is contagious like that, just as her bright personality continues to be. Despite this, the one question on her mind was, *How is it going to get done if this guy won't go get checked out?* A week later, her husband suddenly decided that it's in their best interest to go get tested. The doctors revealed that they had no cause for concern and that, on paper, both of them were as healthy as they could be.

Nine months later, when Joy first spotted that pink line, her breath caught. The world tilted, and before she knew it, her husband was pulling her into his arms, already tearing up. Ore Dayo was conceived.

Her name means "friendship turned to joy." It took six years for Joy's desire to be realized, but there's no arguing that the payoff was huge. The thing to understand from stories like these is that there is nothing, and I mean nothing, that is impossible for our God.

Contagious, Crazy Faith

I want to highlight something truly special from Joy's story, and that's the running theme of intangible things somehow being "contagious." That word feels so negative, especially in the wake of a global pandemic, but I've learned that it's not just the negative that can catch on and spread like wildfire.

While fear, anger, and paranoia can be contagious, so can love, faith, and (pun intended) joy. The Bible calls us to strengthen and uphold one another in faith so that we can endure the trials that define our existence. One of the first things I instantly associated with Joy was—well, her joy! It radiated from a deep place within her. Its presence didn't mean she was free of problems, but it was unwavering and infectious nonetheless. We're called to be contagious in that way so that our joy and faith (though it might be mustard-seed-sized), spreads to the people around us.

In arguably the most influential speech of all time, the Sermon on the Mount, Jesus walks His followers through a set of teachings that are crucial to our philosophy as believers. He says:

13 You are the salt of the earth, but if salt has lost its taste, how shall its saltiness be restored? It is no longer good for anything except to be thrown out and trampled under people's feet.
MATTHEW 5:13 (ESV)

Jesus calls his followers to be seasoning for the earth. Our faith in Him should season this world with goodness. Salt preserves, and in the same way, Jesus wants his followers to be part of preserving the good in this world. Salt is medicinal; Jesus wants us to act as part of the solution and not the problem. We are to be a healing salve against the infection of the human condition.

14 You are the light of the world. A city set on a hill cannot be hidden.
15 Nor do people light a lamp and put it under a basket, but on a stand, and it gives light to all in the house.
16 In the same way, let your light shine before others, so that

they may see your good works and give glory to your Father
who is in heaven.

MATTHEW 5:14–16 (ESV)

Jesus asks us to be a light in this world. A light that, He explains, is meant to be proudly displayed so that it can have a real and positive effect on the people around us. Being the light of the world means being bold enough to let that light show, and in doing so, direct people's attention to the source of that light. Salt and light. It's through these analogies that Jesus laid out how we should be "contagious" in all the best ways.

We let the world's negativity and its darkness infiltrate so much of our lives, but our goal is not to let the world corrupt what's inside of us, but to let what's inside of us change the world. That is the philosophy of Christ. That is the philosophy of joy. Philippians says to rejoice in the Lord always. How do we do this? By understanding our role and place in this world. We are meant to be contagious transmitters of a new philosophy, one that teaches faith in the face of impossible odds. This way, we don't fall into the apathetic mindset that nothing will ever change, that there are some things about our lives or the world that are simply "beyond hope." We are called to be so much more. There's a reason we're called "believers." What defines us is our faith in the One above and the hope for a better tomorrow.

It is this faith that helps women like Joy forgive when it seems impossible. The hurt she had been dealt by her father as a child was immense, and while we're not discussing their conflict at length here, it's important to note that she was able to forgive him many years later only because of the example set by Christ.

She has pledged to take the good from what her parents did for her and discard the bad things she might've endured from their hands. No one is perfect, and it's easy to forget that it's also our parents' first time being human. She wants to take full responsibility for the kind of parent she will be in the hopes that her kids will also live by that example and not find an excuse for any of their future shortcomings in the mistakes she makes. Parental issues have become all too contagious in our world, and it takes the maturity of those who truly understand Jesus's life and message to change that. People like Joy who continue to radiate God's love and peace in every situation. People who are contagious in the best kind of way.

CHAPTER 6

Bait and Switch

He drew me up from the pit of destruction, out of the miry bog,
and set my feet upon a rock, making my steps secure.
    PSALM 40:2 (ESV)

Taking the Plunge

PATRICK WOGLOM FIRST met Julie when she walked into a gym as his client. A personal trainer and a client, a tale as old as time. At first, the two were strictly professional, dating separate people, but the years did their thing. Julie went away to college, they both broke up with their now-exes, and Patrick decided to reach out on a whim. Fast forward a couple of months and . . . *here comes the bride.*

Sometimes the most crippling fears are the ones baked into your very nature as a human being. We're designed to be apprehensive and risk-averse (some of us more than others), and yet so much of our lives revolves around simply "taking the plunge." There's a reason that metaphor works so well. In life, as in a cliff jump, you're rarely in control of how you fall or what you meet at the bottom. There could be palisades of sharp rocks waiting to impale you in those choppy waters down below, or maybe you're in for pristine blue as far as the eye can see. You never really know.

When you're born with a condition that can't be helped, one written into the code of what makes you human, this fear becomes a very tangible monster flowing through your very veins. Julie was diagnosed with familial adenomatous polyposis (FAP) when she was very young, a genetic mutation that, if untreated, almost inevitably leads to colorectal cancer.

She remembers waiting in a hospital gown at twelve, staring at magazines on a waiting room coffee table, while a nurse explained next steps. *Sounds like someone reading out instructions for a broken appliance,* Julie thought. She remembers the bandaging on her lower belly and how, for months after the procedure, she learned to move differently around her scar. Even when it stopped hurting, she found herself adjusting herself to accommodate the ghostly phantom of her operation.

Despite having been treated for her condition and granted the ability to live a relatively normal life so far, it wasn't easy to accept the fact that her very DNA carried something fatal to any future kids. Through high school Julie babysat and nannied for extra cash, all the while pining for a life with children of her own that she wasn't sure she could ever have. FAP is genetic in a very direct way. If one parent carries it, a child has about a 50 percent chance of inheriting it. To Julie, that was 50 percent too many. That "fifty-fifty chance" was more than just some number on a chart, it was a possible life sentence for someone she loved. That fear shaped every conversation about kids. You can certainly understand her apprehension to take the plunge.

Patrick's childhood was almost picturesque. He was an Arizona Catholic boy who attended mass regularly, went to CCD, and spent his weekends playing baseball or blazing through the streets on his Yamaha. Patrick grew up hearing the adoption story the way some kids hear about a family heirloom. He was told it again and again, with small, affectionate details that made it feel like a miracle. He would stand in the kitchen while his mother sliced oranges and painted the scene, recalling the hideous hospital corridors, the couple who signed the papers, and the way his new father lifted him up like he'd finally found lost treasure. These retellings were meant, ultimately, to celebrate. For Patrick, they also did something more. They anchored him to the certainty of being wanted.

For many, the reveal that they are adopted shatters their world, and that reaction is justified and understandable in its own way. But for Patrick, the truth about his birth was never a secret or forbidden knowledge. Instead of being rocked by the sting of abandonment, the certainty of feeling wanted steadied him in a way that was unique. Knowing he had been wanted by somebody gave him confidence and a sense of obligation to live up to that vote of trust. He figured, early, that belonging carried with it a sense of responsibility, and he tried to honor it. As a boy, he volunteered for chores, stayed late to help teachers, and was the first to offer anyone a hand. He didn't do these things out of fear, but out of a wish to be the kind of man deserving of that choosing.

One afternoon at a church picnic, he found himself holding a bawling toddler until the child calmed, his stepfather watching with a small satisfied nod. That image of calm hands, a settled child, and a smile from a man he respected stayed with him. In high school, he took volunteer shifts with kids, coaching rec soccer games and explaining how to tie shoelaces. These simple, unglamorous moments became a kind apprenticeship for the dad he hoped to be one day.

Patrick's adoptive father succumbed to brain cancer when he was ten, but he never forgot the impact simply feeling "chosen" had on him growing up. Everything that he is he owes to his mother and late father. Knowing the difference loving parents made in his life, he decided early on that he *needed* to be a dad. The opportunity he was given couldn't die with him. He would be for another, whether adopted or not, what his late father was to him. This is why when he and Julie got married in 2018, Patrick was more than ready to take the plunge.

Out of the Frying Pan

Another tale as old as time: A faithful woman is often the variable that changes the equation of faith in a man's life. After Patrick left Arizona to study physics at McDaniel College in Maryland, he fell out of the spiritual routine that his father had inspired. His mother was never very religious, but had become ardently less so after the passing of her husband. It wasn't until he started dating Julie that he fell back in love with the faith.

Julie, coming from a life lived in the Brazilian church, decided that she would make the jump to an English one if it meant her husband could come with her. She brought Patrick to her kind of church, one with vibrant music and an atmosphere that exuded joy. He fell in love with the vulnerability of this new kind of service and suddenly became a regular churchgoer once again.

Friction started to develop as Patrick, eager to become a father, struggled to calm his wife's understandable fears about natural birth. She underwent surgery when she was young, and her FAP didn't limit her. There was a good chance it wouldn't limit her kids either. However, knowing that didn't help the anxiety around spreading a generational disease to her children. She didn't want them to go through what she did. She wanted for the FAP in her bloodline to end with her, but that was never going to be a guarantee. Julie's mother, sharing her concerns, was heavily behind IVF. Their anxieties about the risks surrounding natural birth compelled them to research the procedure, but the prohibitive cost caused them to abandon the idea.

One day, a pastor at the church the pair were attending at the time came up to them, somehow knowing of this conflict that existed only behind closed doors. He prayed, telling them to expect a miracle.

Madison was conceived a month later, almost immediately once they had decided to go the natural route. Despite the genetic risk that had weighed so heavily on Julie's heart, Madison was born completely healthy. At the time, there was no indication of complications, and the family felt an immense sense of relief. That said, COVID-era deliveries were far from normal. The hospital was more overwhelming than it used to be, people were all masked up, and visiting hours were limited. The joy of holding a newborn came with a layer of strangeness, as the baby was entering a world still getting back on its feet. People were just beginning to talk to each other again. Restaurants were slowly easing up on social distancing requirements. The future was hardly more uncertain than it was at that time, especially for a young couple. Patrick and Julie remember hoping as they left the hospital that things would get "more normal" by the time Madison was old enough to remember her childhood. How much more normal did it get since then? That's up to you.

The pair lived in complete ecstasy, overjoyed that simply taking the plunge seemed to be all they needed to do. They felt weightless, floating in calm blue waters, not a rock in sight.

Into the Fire

And then came the second child on the way.

They thought they had time, but then one night, Julie woke up with a pain in her abdomen. The emergency room was too bright and the machines too loud. The doctor's words flew by Julie like the sound of planes passing over your house late at night. You can make out just enough to register what's out there, but to your half-asleep mind, it could be a passenger jet or a bomber and it wouldn't make much of a difference.

"Miscarriage . . ."

Huh?

"Observation—"

What?

"... we need to monitor—"

Monitor? Me? Why?

They came home, their growing family now one person smaller.

A sinking feeling. A sucker punch. Sometimes the appearance of one miracle makes everything seem so easy. The elation that comes with the confidence that God is on your side can drain so quickly when a miracle is countered with an unexplained tragedy. It can feel like you got bait-and-switched by God, like He tricked you into believing just to be put back into a place of fear. Is this what faith gets you? It's a scary thing to realize that, as long as you're alive, you're never really "in the clear." Tragedy is a fact of our lives, and this particular strain of tragedy has the potential to destroy faith entirely.

After that, the house seemed to taunt the couple, saying the same thing over and over in different ways. A clean crib still in its box, a tiny outfit still folded and untouched. Grief settled into the small routines of their days. Patrick kept moving, fixing things at odd hours of the night and mowing the yard before dawn because keeping busy was easier than finding the words. Julie drew into herself, staying mostly silent. There were tender moments, sure, but also sharp silences that stung. Over time, a question naturally arose that neither Patrick nor Julie could really answer: How long before we try again?

As time passed, the stabbing pain turned to a dull ache, and the growing Madison kept them plenty busy. A year later, as the family of three were driving to lunch on the banks of Farrington Lake, something caught their eye. The heater hummed, and the radio was on a station that did not demand attention. Patrick's fingers drummed the steering wheel in an even, careful rhythm along to the cookie-cutter radio-pop. Julie sat in the back, covered in crumbs as her daughter picked through an assortment of snacks. Patrick studied the road ahead, as if the answer to the question was printed somewhere on the asphalt. And there it was:

SUNDAY SERVICES

9:00 AM and 11:15 AM

GRACE CHURCH

The words *GRACE CHURCH* on a weathered marquee, letters in block caps like someone had just set down an invitation right before their very eyes.

Patrick made a breathy laugh that was equal parts wonder and fatigue. "That's our girl." Patrick laughed, quietly.

Madison Grace looked up from her sandwich bag of cereal. And she smiled.

Patrick did not pull over and nobody said much, but the couple sat up just a little bit straighter and decided right then and there that Grace Church would be worth a visit the following Sunday.

Do It Again

I don't put my faith in God because He came through once. I put my faith in Him because He has done so time and time again. It was faith in God's ability to come through *again* that made Patrick get up out his seat, take his wife's hand, and march up to the altar for prayer. Now that Julie had tasted motherhood, something she had never thought she would, she wasn't ready to give up on the dream of expanding her family. Patrick knew this.

I remember them coming up. It was the end of a service, and per usual, I made the call for families to approach for prayer, knowing that there was almost always something that somebody needed. Not a single altar call has ever ended with everybody going, "Yeah, we're all good. Thanks for asking." That's why I put the call out there, asking people to be bold and step forward, because I know that all some people need is the invitation.

As people filtered out of the sanctuary and others approached the front, Patrick fumbled with his back pocket like he'd forgotten something. Then, his hand found Julie's. They sat for maybe half a minute more, Julie with her head down, fingers still laced tight in Patrick's. People glanced toward them with the quiet kindness a crowd gives when it doesn't know what else to do.

They stood slowly, Patrick whispering, "We gotta go, Jules."

She squeezed his hand in return.

Patrick led her forward. When they reached the front, they conversed with one of our deacons and were then brought right to me.

I placed my hand on Patrick's shoulder and took Julie's other hand. I did not give a sermon. I named what I saw after having listened to their story. I said, plainly, that I knew what they were carrying was a hard thing and that God knew it too. I said that I knew of the horror of late hours in hospital corridors and late nights spent wrestling with questions we could never answer. And then I said what I always say. "It's done," I whispered to them. "It's a done deal."

A month later, they conceived Mila Grace Woglom. This time, her middle name was no coincidence.

The day she was set to be born, there were a few final scares thrown Pat and Julie's way. Mila, apparently too excited to wait, decided to make her entrance a little early, meaning that the birth plan the couple had agreed on went completely out the window. At the delivery, Mila came out a frightening shade of purple, being strangled by her own umbilical cord. The staff moved like trained dancers, seemingly in rhythm with the monitor that seemed to beep faster by the millisecond. Noise blanketed the room as the doctor flipped from calm into emergency, moving at superhuman speed while nurses called out to one another medical terms that might as well have been a foreign language to the dazed couple. One thing was clear though, there was a chance that either the child or Julie wouldn't make it out of this alive.

For one long breath, the baby was the color of bruised fruit and no sound came from her lips. She wasn't breathing. The hands descended. Somebody clipped the cord, another worked a bulb syringe, a pair of gloves took hold of the tiny torso.

Is my baby going to die? Patrick could hardly breathe himself, thinking of what another death would do to him, Madison, and Julie. And Julie? What if she was the one? What if Mila survived and Julie didn't? *Will another generation have to go through life with just one living parent?*

Patrick's mind ran wild, subjecting him to memories of

watching his dad pass away in a hospital room not unlike this one. If Mila survived but Julie didn't . . . wouldn't that be a cruel twist? A finishing blow. History repeating itself in the lives of his children in a way he never could've imagined. It's hard to stop your mind from spiraling in a case like this, but then he felt that hand. A tug at his heart. *This is faith.*

The cry tore out of her like the breaking of a damn. Patrick went white, then laughed through his tears. Julie's eyes filled with tears of her own as she pressed the small, slick Mila to her chest.

When we step out in faith, we are placing control of our lives in something beyond our comprehension. The person you are today is a complex mash of everyone that's ever impacted you in life and every experience you've ever had. Every moment is the result of a thousand moments before it. Who can truly understand the logic behind why things happen when or how they do? Placing our faith in God doesn't mean we will never have situations in which it's natural to worry. Placing our faith in Him means trusting that whatever we're experiencing is part of a plan to develop us into what we need to be, provided that we love and seek Him with all of our hearts. Sometimes a "bait-and-switch" is really a miracle in the making and a testimony in the trial phase.

CHAPTER 7

The Test

For this child I prayed, and the Lord has granted me my petition that I made to Him.

    1 SAMUEL 1:27 (ESV)

WHEN GOD TELLS you to do something, you only really have two choices. Be obedient or ignore Him, and you should never choose the latter. At least, this is what Alexis has always believed. The thing with God, though, is that sometimes He tells you to do scary things. Scary, nonsensical, and outright illogical things.

Like in 2019, when God told Alexis that it was time to leave her comfortable position as a full-time counselor at a hospital and open up her own private practice. By most people's standards, this was completely illogical at her career stage. You don't leave a stable position on the gamble of a private practice. That's not right! It's common knowledge that you should stay fully employed and build up your private practice on the side till it becomes financially viable. It didn't make sense, but Alexis was faithful to obey. It's a good thing she did, too, because the clients started pouring in. Her Christ-centered approach to mental health, focusing specifically on the struggles of women in crisis, drew a dedicated client base. Soon, the chance she took was already reaping major rewards.

A few months later, Alexis met Derek McGibbon, and . . . you've heard this story about a thousand times. The two got married in May of 2020 and started their life together in the midst of a global shutdown. That virus put these two on the fast track of getting to know each other.

The pandemic wreaked havoc on so many lives, but for this young couple, things were going well. The counseling business that had once felt like a wild gamble was now Alexis's own little baby, a seed she had nurtured and grown into something beautiful. She was excited to watch it continue to grow and experience all that life had to offer with the man she loved. They were blessed from the start, and that was all because of their combined faith in their Creator.

It's not easy to relinquish control of your life to something you can't see, but Alexis has always said she would never not trust God to come through. Whether or not she could stay true to this was to be tested by fire in the coming year.

God doesn't ask for what you can easily give. In October of 2020, just a few months after the wedding, Alexis had a unique experience. As she was praying alone one night, she felt a prompting which she understood to be God whispering to her that it was time to start trying for a child. When Alexis heard this, her heart sank to her stomach. It's not that she never wanted children. In fact, it had always been part of the plan. But while Derek had been ready for a family from the moment they walked down the aisle, Alexis had always envisioned them waiting awhile. *Give me a year,* she told God. One year was all she wanted. One year to navigate the growing pains of married life with her partner. One year to pour her all into her business, a venture that God had blessed. She didn't believe it was convenient to have a kid just then. No, this was *her* year. *Her* year to do the things she wanted. However, there was still her "principle," her life motto, which said that she would never be the one to refuse God's plan. And so, they started trying.

Derek, understandably, was ecstatic to hear Alexis was ready. All his life he had wanted to be a dad, and now that his wife was coming to him, seemingly ready for parenthood, he was over the moon. They began trying in October, but all they saw were negative tests.

The months started ticking by, and with each passing week came more negatives. What was going on? They agreed not to tell anyone, as they didn't want invested third parties in what was, at this point, a prayer known only to the two of them. There would be no begging for prayer on their part. No unsolicited advice from distant family members.

ALEXIS

It's been twelve months. Things aren't adding up.

Is something wrong with me? That's what I keep asking myself on mornings like this, when Derek's still asleep and I'm staring at my reflection in the bathroom mirror, holding yet another negative test. I look down one more time, just to make sure my tired eyes weren't deceiving me. Maybe I'd somehow missed it. Missed that thin, little line that would've changed everything.

Nothing. It was supposed to be there, and it wasn't. Why wasn't it? Am I broken?

No, that can't be right. After all, this baby was God's promise. I know I am whole. I know my body is healthy. God wouldn't promise me something I couldn't have.

Derek and I refuse to see doctors. It's been twelve months. I might be considered infertile. I don't know if I have the faith to believe through a diagnosis like that just yet.

I'm choosing to trust Him, but nothing stings more than when you trust God against the odds and He still fails you. Every night I hear Your voice say, "It's coming. The baby is on its way." Then I wake up and take another test and wonder why You think it's okay to lie to me. There's no baby coming.

I didn't even plan to have a kid. Not now, at least. Would it have killed You to allow me that one year I wanted? These past twelve months spent trying, twelve months of confusion and tears that could've been spent happily. Could You not have given me that time to nurture my business? To grow it like You once asked me to? Could we not have eased into being a couple before you decided it was time to multiply? I didn't want a child then, but You made me want one, and now You won't give one to me.

I'm sorry. I shouldn't be angry. Today just isn't the day.

I toss the negative test and head back into the bedroom. It's early, and even just a half hour of rest would do me some good. But even as I crawl into bed, I have a feeling that I won't be getting any more sleep.

DEREK

There's something so calming about driving. I'm not sure what it is. The trees and grass melt into streaks of green and brown as I barrel down Route 130. The street signs and road markings I've seen a thousand times turn into splotches of red, white, and yellow on the canvas that is the world flying by outside my window. Traveling these roads I've known so well lets me just think.

What can I even do for her? Realistically, not a lot. Alexis said she would be testing today, and she hasn't called or texted, so I'm guessing it didn't go well. What should I say? Should I encourage her? Remind her to believe? Tell her it's okay and that I love her?

Maybe I shouldn't say much. I learned a while back that some days, my silence means more than anything biblical I could spew out. A few weeks ago, as I was trying to decide which of my many solid-color button-ups I should wear to the office that day, I watched Alexis come out of the bathroom with a sullen expression. Her face told me that her soul was tired. We made eye contact for a brief moment.

"Morning," she whispered to me before walking over to the opposite side of the room. Now she was facing away from me, staring at the mirror on our oakwood dresser. I didn't have to ask to know what she had just seen. I thought for a moment about opening my mouth to say something. Something uplifting, something encouraging . . . but then I saw what she was looking at. Pinned to the top-right corner of the mirror with a magnet we got as a souvenir from our honeymoon was a single piece of paper. It was torn right out of my wife's diary, and we had put it up together last week. It said: *FOR THIS CHILD I OBEYED.*

An interpolation of the words of Hannah: "For this child I have prayed." Hannah was a woman in the Bible who desperately wanted a child of her own. She prayed and prayed, and one day, was spotted by a man of God as she broke down in the temple. Long story short, God heard her cries and granted her a son, whom she immediately dedicated to His service. That child was Samuel, a man who went on to become one of the greatest prophets and writers in the Bible.

I didn't know exactly what was going on in Alexis's head, but I knew whatever it was had to do with that verse. The truth is, despite everything, there was still no doubt in my mind that we were going to have this kid. I've always wanted to be a dad, and I know what God has promised. He'd be faithful to fulfill that promise just like He always has. I thought about saying this to her like I have before, but I decided against it.

She didn't need a pastor or motivational speaker. She needed her husband, and maybe what that husband needed to do was say nothing and just understand. She ended up appreciating that more than I could've ever imagined, and so from that day forth, I've grown to value my silence as a comforting tool.

What we both needed was a church. I can't say I don't understand why Pastor decided to close up shop and move to Pennsylvania, but understanding doesn't make it hurt any less. I know the who, what, when, where, and why of our old church's move. It makes total sense in my head, but still.

For people like us who've built our life rhythms around a house of God, the announcement that the church would be relocating was like waking up one morning and finding a room in your house had been boarded over. Maybe there was a logical reason for this. Maybe there was, I don't know, an alligator or something in the room. It makes total sense that you'd want to board up an alligator room. Although, I watched a *Planet Earth* documentary last night and, based on what they said, I'm not sure it would do much good.

This analogy has gotten away from me.

The point is, it felt like the floor had been pulled out from beneath us. We had gotten so used to having the foundation of that particular family to stand on, and now, they were distant. I realize now that that's a much better analogy.

I actually went over to our old sanctuary recently after a tough day at work. The door happened to be cracked open, and the sound of industrial vacuums let me know that the cleaners had left it propped. A sign that the landlords were preparing for the building to be back on the market.

I slipped inside and shocked myself with how much what I saw hurt me. Hymnals piled like abandoned luggage. Furniture stacked to the ceiling on both sides. The sound of vacuuming in the basement. The place was devoid of everyone that had once called this place home. Everyone but me.

Footsteps thudded in the stairwell to the right of the altar. One of the cleaners, sleeves rolled up and face covered in dust, was coming up and out of the basement. "Can I help you, sir?"

"N-no. I'm sorry, I was just leaving."

As I drive home today, I realize tonight might be another difficult night. I don't want her to lose faith, but there's not a lot on my end I can do to help her keep it. There's not a lot about this I can control except the obvious. Besides that, I've been trying to spend this time preparing myself instead of obsessing over Alexis. I realize I'm not yet the ideal man, and I need to work on getting there if I'm going to be a dad. What I need is a full-time job for starters. I've never been a lazy person, but—all right, I won't say I've *never* been a lazy person. I know how to work, but I've always resisted full-time employment. I've always preferred having a lot of things going on at the same time, but I know I need something consistent and stable if I'm going to raise a kid.

There is an "if" there and, although I'd much prefer there wasn't, it has been thirteen months since we first started trying.

I roll to a stop at an empty light. I drum my fingers on the wheel to some nonexistent song as I wait, and my gaze shifts to the right of me. Was this new? No, it had to have been here all this time. It looks weathered. The posts holding it up look like they've been through things.

Planted in the grassy lawn beside the highway are two wooden posts, and suspended between them is a large black banner.

SUNDAY SERVICES

9:00 AM and 11:15 AM

For the first time, I also notice the large brick building just beyond this banner. Across its face is written in bold white letters:

GRACE CHURCH

How come I've never noticed this place before? The light turns green, and the building slowly passes me. We've got to check this place out sometime.

ALEXIS

"Well, what do you think?" Derek whispers to me.

"I like it. It's nice." My hesitation probably makes him feel like I'm not being honest, but I am.

Derek and I decided to come and check out this church because he saw it on his way home from work on Friday. Honestly, I really like it. If it wasn't such a trek from where we live, we might come here more regularly. Everyone's nice here, the worship team is great, and the pastor isn't bad at all. He's been speaking for almost forty-five minutes, and I haven't even felt the time go by. It's a great place, but then again, it is just a *church* after all. I've been in church all my life.

Derek and I are sitting closer to the back. We came in a little late, and these were the best seats we could find that weren't right up at the front. I look over at my husband, and I can't help but smile. Derek's eyes have been glued to the stage since we got here. I think this place just might've found its new biggest fan.

Suddenly, the lights begin to dim and a dull, melodic hum fills the room. When I look back at the stage, the musicians have reappeared from out of nowhere behind the pastor. It looks like the service is winding down.

"Before we leave, we're going to do what we always do here at Grace. We're going to spend some time in prayer. Now, there are days when I'll ask people struggling with certain things to come forward. Finances, marriage, whatever. But today, before you come up, I want you to ask yourself this: What are you believing for?" As the pastor says these words, I feel my chest grow tight. I look at Derek and see that he's already looking at me. I know what he's thinking. On some level, I'm thinking it too, but I never would've found the courage to get out of my seat if he hadn't taken my hand and said—

DEREK

"We need to go up," I say, not allowing myself even a moment to think it through.

"Yes, okay," Alexis responds. "Let's go."

We both get up and march down the aisle toward the open space in front of the stage. We line up next to the others that have come up from the congregation and wait.

An older couple catches our eye from the side of the stage and quickly comes over. They introduce themselves as deacons: Lamont and Denise. Alexis and I are instantly struck by how warm they are. Lamont has a look that seems so sensitive, and Denise radiates warmth in her smile. They ask us about what we are believing for, and I look down at Alexis.

She isn't saying anything. I know what we both want, but I need her to say it. She's been through so much these past few months. She's always prided herself on being obedient, and even though she tries to hide it, I know she feels like God is betraying her. Again, there's only so much I can do. I never stopped believing and I never will, but if this is going to work, I need her to say it.

"A baby." As soon as the words escape her lips, I realize that this is the first time we've ever told anyone about this. I look back at the deacons, who are now looking at each other with determination in their faces.

"Wait here. We'll be right back."

ALEXIS

I left that day feeling like that was the moment. That was the moment it would all change. The deacons brought Pastor Joe to us, and with such incredible confidence, he prayed, "It's done. It's a done deal. You're going to have this baby." That kind of faith grows on you. I felt like I could run through walls.

A few days later, Derek and I spent a free day at the mall. While we were there, we actually bought some baby stuff and put it up on the mantle over the fireplace. I was so sure the prayer had worked!

A few days later, we got another negative reading, and I realized it wasn't a "done deal" in the way I thought it would be. We never stopped buying things. Maybe it was compulsive. Who knows? Every now and then, Derek and I made a trip to a department store and cosplayed being real parents. Bibs and bottles and baby rattles adorn our home. We were so convinced that "this too shall pass," but it's been fifteen months. I've come to hate looking at our little collection on nights like tonight.

We've continued going back to Grace Church from time to time, but I never feel much like praising. The music and sermon wash over me week after week. I can't even say a simple "hallelujah" during worship, even though that's apparently what I'm meant to do.

I remember a dream I had where each of my closest friends held a different weapon. A shield, a sword, a grenade, and an AED (strange, I know) are just a few examples. As I looked around, I felt that each weapon stood for something. Understanding, knowledge, love, etc. Then, I looked down, and in my hands was a flamethrower, and inscribed on it was the word *HALLEL*, a Hebrew word for "praise." Very metal.

Now, I'm no expert at dream interpretation, but there was something real in what I saw. I'm convinced that God, in His own way that night, told me that my weapon was my worship. But how do I praise when I don't feel like it?

I just got off work for the day, and I'm beat. As a counselor, my whole life revolves around being there for women in crisis. When I'm working, I'm usually pretty good at keeping my feelings out of it, but I'd be lying if I said it didn't take a toll on me at times. It's not easy believing for others when you're struggling to even believe for yourself.

I do most of my work on a screen now, with faces in little boxes. You learn to read pauses, the way someone's hand hovers over a cup, the single, shaky breath that comes before a confession. It's delicate work.

There are nights that I log off and still hear a client's small, urgent fear in the stillness of my silent home. There were days I walked into a fertility clinic thinking I had the emotional band-width to hear another test result, only to find I couldn't stop replaying a mother I'd spoken to who'd just miscarried. When a client announced her surprise pregnancy, my first impulse was to celebrate for them. And then, an ugly, private knot tightened in my stomach.

One night I finished with a woman whose voice carried a grief so sharp, it left me feeling dizzy. I had asked her to name one thing she could control this week, and she promised to water the potted plant on her windowsill daily. *There we go! That's progress*, I thought to myself.

I logged off, turned the lamp low, and sat in the glow of my monitor till my coffee went completely cold. My chest heaved the way it did right before I was about to cry. I held myself together out of habit. Out of the obligation to be steady.

Being that voice matters, but doing holy work doesn't make you invincible. I found myself canceling lunch with Derek because a client had an emergency. I was looking over intake forms in the way-too-early a.m.'s and answering crisis texts on Saturdays. Little by little, the margins that I promised I would keep for myself have eroded. I feel not just tired but frayed, like the edge of fabric after way-too-many harsh washes.

I get up from my desk and gently shut my laptop. I need some air. Working from home has its drawbacks. As I start head-ing for the front door, I'm stopped by a faint buzzing coming from the office room. I head back into the office and see my phone's screen lighting up periodically as it vibrates on my desk. I pick it up and answer the call.

"Hey, Mom."

"Hi, sweetie! How are you? How's Derek?" Her voice is sweet and a little frail.

"We're good. You and Dad?" To be honest, I don't feel much like talking right now. I just want to sit outside, melt into our porch chair, turn off my brain, and wait for Derek to come home.

"Oh, we're doing just fine. Listen, I wanted to call you because one of my friends, Vivianne—you know Vivianne, right?"

"Yeah, Mom. I know Aunt Viv." How could I not? I went to school with her daughter for most of my life.

"Right. Well, she's actually been making something for the two of you. And when she told me what it was, I have to say I didn't know how to respond. It looks like you've got some folks back here who want the two of you to get busy." Her voice is a little cheeky now.

"Mom? What are you talking about?"

"Turns out it's not just me who is tired of waiting. Viv's been knitting a blanket for the two of you for five months."

"That's nice of her, but I don't see how—"

"My mistake. It's not actually for you two. It's a blanket for your little one."

When I hear these words, I feel something I can't explain. I had never even told my mother or Aunt Viv about what we were going through. In such creative ways, I'm being reminded by God that the baby is on its way, but at this moment, I can't decide if this makes me happier or just more bitter. I know what God is trying to tell me, and yet, I don't see anything but negative tests.

• ◈ •

Derek and I have decided to steal away to Miami for Valentine's Day. The break has been good for us. The sun, the sand. All of it was therapeutic.

Currently, Derek and I are in our room, unwinding after a long day out on the beach. Derek is sitting on the edge of the bed looking through the room service menu, and I'm lying against the backboard, mindlessly flipping through the few available channels on the room's TV. I'm not really paying attention to the TV. Instead, I just keep turning over the words *make room* in my mind. I've been hearing those words every time I pray.

I grab a notebook out of my suitcase and step out onto the balcony. Miami smells like sunshine and sea salt. It also smells like sunblock and diesel. The heat presses into the bottoms of my forearms as I lean against the railing and think about how tight my life has become. The sweat on my hand makes it hard to keep the notebook from slipping out of my fingers and falling into the artificial palm trees that line the resort's walkways three stories down. It was the notebook that held plans A, B, C, D, and E for when the baby arrived.

And now, I hear something. It's one of those rare times that I'm taking my own advice. I often tell clients to practice setting aside a few minutes a day just to breathe and be still. Right now, in just a couple seconds of doing so, I'm hearing something.

It's no exaggeration that God speaks in a still, small voice. I remember that story of Elijah, who looked for God in miraculous shows of power on a mountain, but ultimately, the voice of God was in the sound of stillness and silence. A whisper on an ocean breeze brought His voice to me today.

God didn't need me to grind more. He was asking me for room. Room to breath. Room to be surprised.

For years I had been building up my counseling practice like the way you build a fire when you're cold. More sessions! More clients! More hours! I told myself it was obedience, and in large part, it was for the season I was in then. I told myself that God had opened the door and that I should walk through it. That was also true, in part.

The problem is, my life is built in a way that isn't conducive to the baby we're trying to have. What did more clients, more hours, and more sessions mean if they all existed to provide for a baby that I wouldn't spend a lick of time with? Right now, in this moment, as my eyes trace a freighter slowly gliding along the distant horizon, God is asking me to do something. He's not asking me to abandon what I've built, but to make room in the life I've become a little addicted to for Him. To make room for that baby I claim I'm believing in.

I guess God is a big believer in sustainability. I open up the notebook and thumb through the schedules I've written down. The marketing plans and expansion strategies I had penciled into pages immediately following ones that contained notes on birthing methods and private schools in the area. It was a mess, like my mind was a mess about all of this. A tangible representation of the disgusting hybrid between work and life that my brain had been getting too familiar with. I shut the notebook and go back inside. This wasn't sustainable. I needed to throttle back.

"Should I stop counseling?" I can't believe what I'm saying.

Derek's head whips around to face me. He's got a bewildered look on his face. "Stop counseling? What happened? You don't want to anymore?"

"It's not that. I love it."

"But what's wrong, then?"

"Well, if I'm going to be a mom. I can't be working all these hours, can I?"

The truth is, I'm more than burnt out at this point. I'm both managing my practice and working full-time as a counselor. I am essentially the business's founder, manager, and lead counselor all at the same time.

I don't know if I still fully believe God is going to come through. He keeps giving us these reminders, these demands, these requests. I listen to them all. I'm who He wants me to be, and He still won't bless me. I'm getting ready to sacrifice a part of this passion project God told me to build. He told me to start it, and now I'm getting ready to loosen my control over it just for this hypothetical child that's supposedly coming.

But I've always been obedient.

I'll start by turning off the targeted ads that have been pulling in clients at the margins. The second we're back in Jersey, I'll call our practice manager and cut as many of my weekly slots as I, and the other therapists, can manage. I wouldn't be giving up the business entirely, but restricting myself to an exclusively managerial role. Next week, I'll begin the process of handing my clients over to those who work for me. In short, I'll be restructuring my hours in a way that would reflect what they would look like if I was pregnant.

DEREK

It's early March, and I'm sitting at the dining table in Pastor Joe's house. I've never been one for small groups, but I heard about this "Dreamer's Roundtable" that Pastor was running one Sunday, and I decided to check it out. If for no other reason, then at least for that incredible name.

It's a group designed for men from all walks of life to come together and talk freely about their lives, struggles, and dreams. Pastor's been asking each of us to set some goals for the next month, as well as a game plan for how we'll achieve them. After all, wishful thinking isn't a strategy.

I heard a bunch of different goals. Some men want to take their wives out more. Others want to commit to spending a few more hours each week with their kids. As for me? I want to do three things before March ends. I want to read three books, finally change Alexis's last name to mine (it's a long story, but basically, quarantine weddings can be a pain), and lastly, I want that baby.

Pastor smiles at me. "That's quite a list, Derek. But you haven't told us your game plan."

"Well, that's where it gets a little complicated. For the books, I know exactly how many pages I need to read a day to get them done. For the name change, I have appointments I need to make. As for that last one, there's not much I can do aside from practice, practice, practice . . ."

ALEXIS

I'm sitting in the car, gripping the wheel so tight, I think I'm choking it. I'm parked under a parking lot lamppost and keep my hands on the wheel because moving seems impossible at a time like this. I was supposed to run in, grab a thing for Derek's birthday, something small and useful, but now I can't remember what I meant to buy.

Seventeen months at this point. Is this some kind of sick joke? Is this funny to God somehow? Here I am, red with anger because God won't give me a baby I wouldn't even have wanted if it wasn't for Him in the first place. What is left for me to do? What command haven't I obeyed? What request haven't I followed to the letter? What else do I have left to give You?

I'm sure I've done the right thing, and I've been holding my fears at arm's length, distracting myself with all the planning I could do. But tonight? The levee's broken, and the floodwaters have come roaring in. The pit in my stomach feels like a stone I can't move.

The radio spins a song I don't know. There is an honesty in the voice of the singer that makes me sit straighter. He isn't polishing the words. He says them almost like he's surprised to find the words in himself. Gratitude. He sings about simple, stubborn gratitude. I turn it up because I want to hold on to anything that isn't my own thinking.

Gratitude. The word lands like a small raindrop on my hand, and I realize there's something I've been holding back. I have been obeying instructions and measuring outcomes and bracing for the next fault line. What I haven't done is praise. I have been too busy to speak directly to the thing I desperately want and thank the One who can give it. I've been worshiping results. Not God.

Gratitude. Radical, rebellious gratitude.

Gratitude in advance.

I don't plan it. The tears come first, hot and surprising, and then my throat opens in a sound that is half sob and half song. I say the names of things out loud. The practice, Derek's laugh, the women who I can call at one in the morning. The list is messy.

Then I stop trying to format it into a prayer and say the plain things. The words are clumsy and ridiculous and true. I promise nothing grand. And then I sing.

Hallel.

Like Paul and Silas, singing while chained up in the belly of a prison, singing like they didn't care if God brought them out or allowed them to stay there, I sing.

I sing, *really*. I mouth the words quietly under my breath, and they begin to force themselves out with greater conviction word by word.

The surrender I make is embarrassingly ordinary, and yet my vision is clouding into watercolor.

It's not as if the sky splits open or anything. The praise is not dramatic. I don't levitate or have a vision of the heavens opened. I simply let my voice do what it couldn't for months—worship like I meant it. The shape of the prayer is simple and strange. It's not about bargaining. It's not a list. It is a raw, tiny offering of thanks.

The tightness behind my eyes eases a fraction. The roar in my head quiets. For a moment, the wanting and the waiting sit beside each other without fighting. Perhaps they've both been silenced by the arrival of a newcomer. Gratitude.

The song finishes, and the DJ moves on.

I'm sitting here in this lot, fully bawling now.

DEREK

It's March 23, a day before my birthday. This week has been good for me. I landed that full-time position I was looking for! By next week, I'll be the staffing director for a few shipping facilities in North Jersey. I can't wait to tell Alexis.

Speaking of which, where is she? I'm walking around the house now, calling her name, and I'm hearing no response. I enter our empty bathroom and spot something that makes my heart twinge with pain. A negative test. She must've left it out by accident. At this point, she doesn't really bother with showing me them.

I let out a sigh and head back out to the living room, where I fall into our favorite couch. Directly in front of me is our "vision mantle." Hang on, I know that sounds kind of New Age-y. Let me explain.

Over the past six months, we've been collecting items in faith and putting them around our fireplace. It began on a rainy Saturday last year when we decided we'd head out to a mall and just go shopping. Not for groceries or toiletries or furniture. Just clothes and other stuff like that. We spent the day there, just browsing and eating various fatty fried foods in the food court. And then, at one outlet, Alexis picked up a tiny Giants jersey. That was the start of it. I fumbled for a bib with bears.

We came home that night giddy and laid out what we'd bought on our mantel like trophies. Thus, the "vision mantle." We were buying things in faith for our baby-to-be, reminding ourselves physically that this was going to happen. The collection started small, a private thing we could visit when we were running low on hope, but over time, it grew.

Baby clothes, bibs, rattles, shoes, etc. I've always been a big visual representation guy. I love vision boards and to-do lists. When our hopes were high, we would go out and buy little symbols of the promise and put them up so that we would never forget what was coming. It's honestly a little sad how big it got.

It was all well and good till about two weeks ago, when I started noticing things missing. First, it was the bib with little bears. The next morning, our mini Giants jersey was gone. Then, a rattle. Daily, something else would be stowed away. I asked Alexis about it once and got cold-shouldered. I let it go. It's not like I really needed an explanation. Some things just get too painful to look at. Like that piece of paper that used to be on our mirror that I found in the trash last month.

Today, it was officially empty. The last item, a pair of baby shoes, had been discarded.

I hear the door leading to our backyard patio slide open with a dull *screech*. Alexis comes inside and reclines on the couch with a look that says she's surprised to see me.

"Oh, hey there, handsome! Home so early?" She's smiling. Not just in a polite way, either. It's a genuine, radiant smile.

Weird. "It's six o'clock. I'm always home at this time."

"It's six o'clock?" She looks over at the clock on our mantle. "Looks like it is! That's funny!"

"Yeah, funny. Are you doing, all right? How was your day?" It's not that I don't like how happy she seems. It's just that I don't see where it's coming from.

"Awesome! In fact, I took some time to put together a little something for you."

"For me? But my birthday isn't till—"

"Tomorrow, I know. But I just couldn't wait. I have two gifts for you this year, and you get to pick one to open early." She holds out two closed fists and looks right into my eyes. "Go ahead, pick one."

I don't know what's going on here. I tentatively tap her right hand, but instead of revealing what's inside it, she just nods and disappears back into the bedroom.

"Alexis? Where'd you go?" I call after her.

"I'll be back in a minute." She is indeed back in a minute, with a big purple gift box in her hand.

"Whoa, what's this?" I ask, completely dumbfounded.

"Go ahead," she says, pushing the box onto my lap. "Open it."

I slowly unravel the gold ribbon that had been tied around the box and then slide off the cover. Inside, I see the items Alexis had been taking from our mantle. The shoes, the bib, the jersey. Everything is in it.

I don't know what happened, but I take it this is her way of telling me that she's ready to start believing again.

"This is incredible, babe. I'm so proud of you. You have no idea how much it means to me that you're ready to believe for this again, 'cause I haven't lost faith, and I just know that—" I start talking, practically bursting at the seams with joy, but the expression on Alexis's face tells me I've missed something. She's still smiling at me, but her eyes say that I haven't gotten it yet. What am I missing?

"Derek." She's still beaming from ear to ear.

We sit in silence for a minute before it finally clicks.

"This—this is . . . you're pregnant?" The words leave my throat in bits and pieces, like a part of me didn't want to get my hopes up too high.

She nods yes. I'm left speechless. Best birthday ever.

Conclusion
Burnt

Church-burnt people have a certain aura about them. What does it mean to be church-burnt? Well, we typically use the word to describe those who are experiencing extreme exhaustion (physical, mental, emotional, or spiritual) caused by overinvolvement in church activities or other ministerial obligations. These are the battle-worn Christians. The ones that made their bones in the church. The ones that have served faithfully, whether as singers, musicians, ushers, greeters, or anything else that falls under the umbrella of ministry work. Church burnout affects so many more people than you realize, because they feel intensely guilty about admitting that they have grown "weary in doing what is good." That phrase comes from the book of Galatians, where we're encouraged not to lose heart in doing right. But somewhere along the way, many Christians came to believe that needing rest is the same thing as disobedience. Those Christians push themselves to the bone, with zero breaks to pull back and rest, until fatigue turns to bitterness and resentment. Before they know it, they begin to resemble the hardened and callous church folk some of you might unfortunately associate with God's kingdom.

This was never how Jesus intended His followers to live. In fact, He preached that a continuous and overflowing sense of peace and love should define all of our actions. If you feel that you're being worked to the limit in God's kingdom, it's important you take stock of your spiritual health and see if a break wouldn't do you some good. Sometimes, those in ministry are so driven by their need to be "doing things" for the kingdom that when their home church suddenly ceases to exist, they are unsure of what to do. Years' worth of tiredness and confusion suddenly hit them when they are abruptly forced to grind to a halt.

Derek and Alexis's home church before Grace made a drastic move to a different state. The emotional and spiritual capital they had invested in this church left them feeling unsure of what their next steps were.

It wasn't anger so much as it was surprise that took them. Or maybe it's better described as a small, tight disappointment that lives in those who watch the things they trusted in quietly dissolve. The church didn't crumble due to drama or offense. It didn't disband due to a lack of attendees. No, this was simply a tactical, strategic decision to relocate to a state that better served the leadership. There wasn't a place where fingers could be pointed, no one to bear the blame. All that remains when you've sifted that out is a nagging feeling of abandonment.

I found out about some of this later on, but when they first approached me for prayer, I could already read that they were seasoned believers. More importantly, they were seasoned believers that harbored some kind of hurt or burnout involving the church. Praying for people like this does sometimes, I'll admit, make me nervous.

I got the impression that they were good, solid people who loved God and had a deep heart for service. I understood it might take some time for them to warm up to regularly serving again, but a break was just what the doctor ordered for them anyhow.

After praying for them, I would often talk to God. I would say, "Please, just let this one happen quickly. I know they have You in their lives, but they need this right now. I have to believe it's Your will."

They usually sat in the back, so I didn't get to see them much while preaching, but I would always make an effort to ask whenever I did speak to them. One day, they caught me by the altar after having just concluded a service.

"Pastor Joe? Do you have a minute?" Derek asked as he shook my hand.

"Oh, hey, Derek, Alexis," I replied. "Yeah, I guess I do."

"We need to talk to you." Derek said, his face looking grim.

I started sweating bullets. I'd yet to have a good conversation that started out this way. You don't say that when you want to have a friendly chat. You say that when you want to punch someone in the face or at least call them out for doing something terribly wrong.

Did I say something wild in today's sermon? No, that wasn't it. My mind raced as they led me to the back of the building and into our then-empty broadcast studio. *Oh, boy. Here we go.*

I braced myself for a difficult, uncomfortable conversation as Alexis began looking through her bag. Suddenly, I saw Derek crack a smile. *Weird,* I thought.

Alexis pulled out something and placed it in my hands. It should've clicked immediately. I'd had six kids after all, but for some reason, my brain was buffering that day. It was a positive pregnancy test in a sealed plastic bag. When I realized what I was holding, a thousand worries turned into pure joy. A lot of tears followed. Happy tears.

Hallelujah

The word *hallelujah* literally translates to "praise Yah." In Hebrew, *YHWH* (often rendered *Yahweh*) is the personal name of God. The word *hallelujah* combines *hallel*, meaning "to praise," with God's personal name. It is a powerful liturgical expression that has been used for centuries to convey a deep-seated sense of joy, gratitude, and praise to the living God. I wanted to take a moment and unpack Alexis's experience with this.

I'm a huge proponent of the idea that worship can directly translate to breakthrough. This idea has a foundation in scripture. One of my favorite passages in the Bible is in the second book of Chronicles, where King Jehoshaphat places the priestly worship leaders in front of his military as they advance upon a camp of enemy invaders. This might seem like poor military strategy, but they were demonstrating for the generations the power of complete faith in God combined with a culture of praise. They went forward while singing and glorifying God, saying, "Praise the Lord, for His mercy endures forever!" By the time the Israelites reached the enemy camp, they found it completely defeated. God had caused the three enemy kingdoms to suddenly turn on one another. The enemies of the Lord had destroyed themselves in a frenzy while His faithful, with their attention placed squarely on His goodness, had to do nothing but worship their way to a victory.

We praise God because He deserves it. We praise God because in doing so, we find restoration and breakthrough. Faith is the key factor in every story of a miracle, and praise is one of the deepest expressions of undying faith we are capable of as human beings. In praise, we uplift God with our voices and enthrone Him in our hearts. We sing with gratitude even though our circumstances might not seem to call for it. By cultivating a habit of praising God even when it makes no sense, we free our souls and demonstrate our trust in Him. When I choose to praise the Lord despite my circumstances, I'm saying, "I don't care what may come. I don't care what the world throws at me. I stand here, unashamed and unafraid before my God. And I know for a fact that He is good to me."

Alexis knew that she had been gifted with an innate desire to praise. It was through this that her spirit felt closer to God. For the many months that her faith was attacked, she felt unable to truly trust and therefore praise Him. When she finally let loose and resolved to march toward that enemy encampment with her praise leading the way, the doors opened up.

CHAPTER 8

Surrender

Behold, children are a heritage from the Lord,
the fruit of the womb is a reward.
    PSALM 127:3 (ESV)

The Perfect Day

CLACK! TROY WATCHED as the small white ball, launched by his driver, soared through the air and spun over the rolling hills, which stretched out before him like the grand folds of a lush, green fur throw. The sun's warming golden rays combined with the gentlest of breezes that cooled the droplets of sweat that had accumulated on Troy's brow. It was indeed a perfect day out on the course.

He swiped a white, gloved hand over his brow.

Okay, a few degrees cooler, and then . . . then it would've been perfect.

It was bright, the kind of bright that exposed everything and seemed to burn away all shadows. The grass seemed to glow emerald as it attempted to throw the sun's rays right back at it, bathing the course in vivid color. An almost comic-book-like world lay open before Troy, and it was his. And it was still.

For these few hours, Troy was allowed to be still.

His ball had turned into nothing but a speck of white about two hundred yards ahead on the expanse of green before him. Troy stood with the driver in hand, and you could see how the sweeping horizon could make a man feel small. The kind of small that gets him talking to God about the big questions. As many great saints can attest to, silence is God's first language.

Thousands throughout the history of the church have found nature and silence to be the golden combination that stirs up a need to speak to God. It's in the stillness that they would meditate and pray for hours.

Tapping into this ancient tradition (without intending to, I should add), Troy began to whisper under his breath. "God, is this what it feels like to be without children?" Troy shielded his eyes from the sun and began to walk forward, lost in thought.

There's something to be said about this whole "wisdom of the ancients" thing. With how exhausting our daily lives have become, it's no shock that the moments people tell me they've heard from God the most clearly are moments just like these. God speaks in the mundane, the simple, the still. It was when Troy was focused on nothing but his environment, the susurration of his golf shoes on the grass as he walked, and hitting the perfect drive that God decided to prick his heart.

"Troy!"

He moved farther, unconcerned with a particular direction.

"Troy, wait up!"

By all accounts, life was good. What more could a guy want? He was successful in a profession he loved, had good friends, and had a good relationship with God. He even had time to *golf* on the weekends! According to most bachelors, this is the closest you can get to heaven on earth.

"Troy! Hey, Troy!"

Troy was certainly no slouch when it came to ministerial life either. His life had been defined by God, by ministry. He had spent his childhood in the church, volunteering and hanging out with the youth group. He was a worship leader and came from a family with a rich history of service in God's house. He had spent his life cultivating a deep prayer habit and a personal connection with Him, and yet . . .

"Hey, man, were you planning on waiting for us?"

Troy jumped as a buddy clapped him on the shoulder. He turned around and faced his friends, a little shocked at how far he'd wandered from where he'd begun.

For about ten minutes, Troy had forgotten he had come here with anybody.

Troy and his friends spent the rest of the afternoon having a great time, sipping cold drinks while they talked and laughed. It should've been a perfect day, but the logistics of this "fatherhood" thing worked at Troy.

He wasn't young. In fact, he was nearing his forties. He had been told all his life that at the right time, a woman would come into his life. She hadn't. He had been told that fatherhood was *the thing* to look forward to as a man. But here he was, killing it on the course, wondering if that was even still a possibility for him.

The "On-Time God"

You'll find somebody special. God has someone just for you. Just hang in there; you'll meet "the one."

So Troy had been told all his life. At twenty, he stood as a groomsman at wedding after wedding and toasted friend after friend. At thirty, he moved apartments and painted rooms alone on Saturday mornings while churchmates his age talked about kids in the fellowship hall on Sunday afternoons. At thirty-nine, he celebrated a nephew's birthday and felt that odd mixture of joy and a private ache. People meant well, telling him not to worry. They always do, don't they? But the words can start to grow hollow as the years tick by. Trusting God is one thing. It's another to sit with this kind of particular, slow grief of postponed plans.

God rarely operates on our timing. He moves in the background to line things up so perfectly that when everything comes together, we have no choice but to ascribe to God his due credit. Sometimes, He'll work things out in this way to keep us from becoming too assured in our own strength.

Troy was raised in upstate New York in a "God" family. His grandparents were ministry leaders, his mother served like a saint at his local church, he started leading worship in his teens, and he connected with his two lifelong best friends at youth group. His life was so tied to the church that when he was given the opportunity to use his college degree in physical therapy and personal training to open a gym of his own, something he had dreamed of since he was a child, he was hesitant because it felt like his career should be more "God-centric." With how much time he had spent in the church, it's understandable that he should feel strange stepping into this seemingly unrelated field. By this time, he had also been certified at an accredited theological institution. *Should I be opening a church?*

I immediately sympathize with anyone with the specific kind of insanity needed to even consider church planting. I was that guy, and though it's worked out well for me, there's no way I can in good conscience recommend pastoral life. It's endlessly trying, but, to be fair, just as rewarding. Do with that what you will.

Fortunately, Troy understood something crucial before making that leap. It's something I'd like all of you to understand as well.

Here's the thing: Doing life with God doesn't necessarily mean you become a preacher or open a church. There are millions of Christians around the world. If each one of them decided that being close to God meant that they had to open a church, we would have more Sunday services than we'd know what to do with. Troy was given this gem by some of his spiritual mentors: "You asked God for direction, and He gave it to you. You've wanted to run a gym since you were a kid, and now God's making it happen. If you let Him, maybe He can make your gym your church."

Troy opened up his facility, and eventually, met that girl he'd been promised.

Imagine landing in a place where the letters on street signs might as well be hieroglyphs and your pockets hold a couple hundred bucks and nothing else. That was Tatianna. I've heard the story enough times to know that the details matter—her birth under the Iron Curtain, her departure from Russia, the long bus rides, her first American paycheck that she tucked away like a treasure, the nights she practiced English using radio shows and sitcoms until the words grew clearer.

Tatiana came to America carrying with her a tenderness for children, especially orphans, from her homeland. Here, in America, was Troy, a lifelong ministry man longing for children. Coming to meet him from the opposite side of the planet was a woman who had forever loved kids, like Jesus did, and dreamt about helping them.

Now, married to Troy and living here in America, she designs and helps run orphanages back home in Russia for underprivileged children. She has worked on dozens of them.

After many failed "flirt-to-converts" in Troy's youth and a lot of relationships that just didn't feel right, meeting Tatianna felt completely refreshing. They bonded over their mutual love for God and cultivated their relationship through prayer. When Troy would bring up difficulties in his day-to-day, Tatianna would suggest praying together. You'd be hard-pressed to find a better sign of good things.

Months into their relationship, on a night when the gym lights were low and the last client's echoes had faded, Troy and Tatiana stood with their cups of coffee and prayed aloud. Exhausted and fatigued beyond measure, they prayed a simple, non-showy prayer. They asked that God would help them love what they did, and help them to find rest in it.

They left that night with a confidence that felt different from anything Troy had known. It might be a little cliche, but even I can testify to the power of "when you know, you know."

For Troy, that kind of quiet, caffeine-scented prayer was the kind of knowing that stuck.

They would call each other every night to pray, and sometimes, just sit in silence. All three of them. Troy, Tatianna, and a God who loved them both. Sometimes that's all we need, to sit in a moment where everything melts into background noise. It's a great sign when you find someone who helps usher you into that kind of peace of mind.

Troy and Tatianna got married when many said that it was "too late in life" to be doing so. Many said that kids were certainly out of the question at this age, but they started trying regardless. Originally, Troy didn't foresee much of a challenge.

While God doesn't operate on our timing, neither does biology. At this point in reading, you might've picked up on that already. The truth is, for men and women in their forties, conception can sometimes take longer, tests can yield more complications, and there are extra conversations to be had with doctors. Those realities don't cancel out faith, but they do change the emotional landscape.

The next few months came in sharp, small episodes. Month one brought the first negative result. Month three was memorable as the first time a nurse said the words, "We'll run tests." Month five was marked by night after night of bitter, yet optimistic prayers. Month seven, and most of that optimism seemed to have been drained from them.

A younger couple would've had the mental fortitude to keep hoping, perhaps. But this whole thing was turning into a kind of sick "you're too old" joke. Troy and Tatiana had waited so long for "the right one." It was what they'd been told to do.

Was that wait going to be the thing that killed their dream of parenthood?

Eight months later, Troy realized that perhaps having a kid in his forties wouldn't be as easy as he thought. He got himself tested, and as expected, his body was nowhere near as ready to have kids as it would've been in his twenties.

Surrender

We get so wrapped up in understanding why life doesn't happen the way we want it to that we miss the importance of total surrender, leaving everything in God's hands, and embracing the struggle. Troy was given an especially vivid example of what surrender looks like in his youth when he watched his mother, the most diligent woman he knew, struggle as his father suffered a brain aneurysm and proceeded to live as a paraplegic for the rest of his life. One of the most selfless, pious, kindhearted people in his world was being slowly broken by life's challenges. That was the first time he could ever remember being mad at God. *Why me? Why us? After everything we've done for You. After everything my mother and our family have given up for Your house. Is this what You wanted?*

Troy told me about the night he sat on the kitchen step and watched his mother lift his father's bowl to his mouth. The house smelled like boiled potatoes and antiseptic. He heard a low melody and saw that his mother was singing under her breath. It wasn't a hymn he'd ever heard. Perhaps it had only been written on her heart for this moment. That day, Troy saw a kind of faith that didn't need fanfare. It worked to serve and kept on serving. It didn't answer his questions about fairness, but it taught him what it meant to carry a difficult cross with grace. That memory stayed with him when he would later wrestle with his fears surrounding parenthood. How was he to carry something that God had given him without turning resentful? His mother's actions reached forward in time to give him an answer. His mother's prayer became his own: "If this is the cross you're having me bear, then give me the strength to carry it."

There's no doubt that children are a huge blessing, but I've seen that sometimes letting go of a desire that close to your heart can be equally as freeing as seeing those prayers answered. We must be dedicated to our prayer for the things we want, but also be open to hear the voice of God, who has nothing but the best in mind for us. He knows our frame, our strengths, and our weaknesses. Our days and our paths have been marked out by Him, and our job is to surrender to the current rather than fight it. He has a good life to show you if only you will let Him. That life might not be the one you've pictured, but under His direction, it's no doubt the one you want to be living.

Tatianna and Troy laid everything at God's feet. Whatever His answer, they resolved in their hearts to be satisfied. If kids weren't for them, so be it. They would instead look forward to the unique calling God had waiting for them.

They had no idea that the "On-Time God" was already moving on their behalf.

Gains, God, and Grace

A man walked into Troy's gym one day. He was wearing a T-shirt that said, *Grace Church.*

I know Grace Church, Troy thought as he watched him walk in. An old friend and spiritual mentor of his, Charles Jackson, was now at Grace Church. Get this, Troy had also been longtime friends with Charles's daughter, who is now married to my son. It's a small world, isn't it? You can already see how God had been pulling it all together. He set this in motion many years ago when Troy's family and Charles's family first started serving Him together.

Troy struck up a conversation with the Grace-man, who he came to find out was running the church's youth group. Troy remembered how, when he was growing up, his youth group would host basketball nights at local gyms and high schools to keep kids off the street. Those nights gave him some of his fondest childhood memories. At that moment, the advice Troy had been given about his gym becoming a "church" of sorts came flooding back into his mind. Troy told the man that he was free to bring his youth group over on Saturdays after hours to work out, play basketball, or help themselves to the protein bar. He suggested that they could even hold a small worship set with a devotional in the aerobics room.

The two talked for a while and went their separate ways, and later that week, Troy ended up speaking to Charles for the first time in a decade. The conversation flowed as if they'd never been out of contact. Eventually, they wound their way to the topic of family and children. That's when Charles mentioned the special anointing Grace Church has when it comes to couples and conceiving.

Troy and Tatianna came to get a feel for our church during a midweek service. Troy later remarked that if he had felt something "off" with our kind of service, he would've left and never looked back. Understandable. You don't want just *anybody* praying for you, after all. He trusted the opinion of a man he looked up to, but he did his due diligence as a husband and man of God.

They came back as a pair on Sunday and found me. Now, it's important that we pause here and understand just how strange the kind of "prayers" discussed in this book can feel, especially to someone coming from a life of church. Troy was used to longer, verbose, and passionate prayers. He later remarked that as I began, he "dug his heels into the ground" in preparation for an "anointed pastor" to pray a dense, Old Testament-style blessing. You can imagine his shock when it was all over in a few seconds.

"It's done? It's done! Can you believe that? That's all he said. He said, 'It's done,' and that was it!" Troy was still trying to process what had happened as he drove home, talking on the phone with his close friend, another pastor named Joe. After a brief pause, Pastor Joe burst into laughter.

"It's done, huh? Well, he called it. If he said it's done, it's done! Somehow, someway, you're having that baby,"

Troy heard the faith and joy in Joe's voice. In seconds, he started to feel it too.

There's nothing wrong with a good, long prayer. I love them myself. All us "spiritual" people do, but there's something to be said about simplicity when you're asking something of God. It is faith that makes all the difference, not necessarily long-winded prayers or passionate speech. At first, Troy was almost upset because he didn't hear what he expected. However, as has been said time and time again, our expectations are often the greatest obstacles to what God can do. Jesus left His own hometown of Nazareth because the townsfolk lacked the faith needed for Jesus to even perform miracles there. Miracles aren't always a prerequisite for faith but are often a byproduct of it.

Think of how Jesus declared things in faith. A few words from Him are all it took to cast out demons, transform lives, and control the natural world as we see it. The reason I pray in this way is because, for me, there is zero doubt in my mind that God will pull through. Faith as small as a mustard seed can move mountains. I think we're all on a lifelong journey to accumulate just that much.

It's not easy to put your complete trust in something you can't see, but I can personally witness that the invisible God has shown up in very visible ways in my life. While I have yet to see His face, I see the evidence of His love in my life every single day.

The prayer he received might not have been what he came expecting to hear, but the results speak for themselves. Troy never thought he would have a son, and now he does, with a second child on the way.

CHAPTER 9

Miracles of Circumstance

For as the heavens are higher than the earth,
so are My ways higher than your ways
and My thoughts than your thoughts.
    ISAIAH 55:9 (ESV)

God-Incidence

BECAUSE WE'RE TRAINED to look for God in the spectac-
ular and the impossible, we often miss the evidence of Him
working in the "improbable." It's been said many times, but
God is less of a magician in our day-to-day lives and more of
a "backstage operator." He orchestrates things at a level far
above what we can ever comprehend, but because we're so
focused on extravagant shows of power, we fail to realize the
million little miracles that allow us to lead the lives we do on a
daily basis. Miracles that are by the provision of God for those
that love Him. Sometimes we even rob God of the gratitude
He deserves because we ascribe His work in our lives to "coincidence." Granted, sometimes life just throws you a bone, but

in learning to open our eyes to the power of faith, we realize that many of these instances of favor are not coincidences, but God-incidences.

For many families, an inability to have kids isn't their biggest concern. They say, "I can physically have kids now, but I don't see how it's going to work because of my circumstances, and if I put it off long enough, I might never have any."

Extenuating circumstances can be financial, a lack of time, distance, etc. Of course, we must be responsible with when and how we choose to bring children into the world, but this story advocates the power of trusting in God to navigate difficult circumstances.

It's important to hear stories of not just the impossible being made possible, but of God working to give those who love Him the desires of their heart even when it seems highly *improbable*. Sometimes all we need in life is a miracle of circumstance. This was especially true for Krissy and her husband, Eric, whose journey to parenthood involved the obstacle of the US Armed Forces.

Eric, Krissy, and Uncle Sam

Despite having survived an incredibly difficult and abusive childhood, Krissy's attitude toward having a child was (some say, "surprisingly") positive. She wanted a child of her own, not so that it would "heal" her, but so that she could finally give what she had never received. No one had tucked her in at night, shielded her from harm, or made her feel safe. She had a noble wish to reverse that narrative, to have a child and make sure that they never doubted that they were cherished.

Krissy would eventually leave her home due to an intensifying abusive situation and move in with her boyfriend, Eric, whom she had met in a study hall at Rider University. Eric's family was more than happy to take her in, and having found a stable home for the first time in her life, she began to explore religion.

I've always believed that God has placed a kind of homing beacon in the human heart. In Ecclesiastes, scripture says that God has "put eternity into man's heart." When the world around us collapses and nothing makes sense, that beacon starts to stir. It's like a compass, pointing us in the right direction.

For Krissy, the pain of her past and the sudden stability of Eric's home awakened in her a longing she couldn't explain. For the first time in her life, she was allowed to ask the big questions. She was allowed to wonder about God and what happens when we die rather than simply being caught up in surviving the day-to-day. Removed from a trauma-packed home life and in a space that supported her wonder, she was finally free to recognize the gentle pull of that homing beacon. She began to research on her own, diving through the history and of course, the theology of the Christian church. The internet is a powerful thing, and it gave her a place to start. Hearing about this reminded me of what I was like when I first gave Christianity a real try and went full Indiana Jones, specifically looking into archaeological sources that confirmed biblical events. It's in this chapter of her life, as she was bubbling over with divine curiosity, that she first began attending Grace Church.

I wish I could explain exactly how it works, how a human heart can be so radically changed, but within a few months, Krissy (previously a staunch atheist) became a regular at Grace

Church. I would often see her sitting by herself in service and leaving the second it ended. Not much of an extrovert. People assume pastors don't notice these things in their congregation when they're up onstage, but we're more observant than you would think. It's always nice to see someone gradually warm up to the house of God.

Having found an anchor in Jesus, Krissy's mental state improved. Parental abuse comes with heavy chains, and in my experience, the breaker of said chains is found within the four walls of a church and the pages of the Bible. Around the same time, Krissy made a radical decision that most who knew her would never have been able to predict. She was going to join the Air Force.

To her, the military looked like order after years of chaos. It was structure, stability, a way to prove that she could stand on her own, and a meaningful opportunity to truly make a difference.

Apparently, on her first Sunday at Grace, I had touched heavily on the miraculous conceptions we had been seeing around that time. Many young couples who had thought themselves unable to conceive were giving shocking testimonies (some of which are included in this very book). That day, as she listened to me preach about God opening impossible wombs, she decided that maybe He could also carry her into an uncertain future. That future was made all the more "uncertain" by the fact that this message came just as she and her boyfriend had begun planning for their future family.

The Air Force would be a massive hurdle to overcome. She married her boyfriend, who eventually decided to join the Navy, and now the two of them were really in a bind. Many military folk start building families when they're young, but if the two of them were going to join separate divisions within a short window, who knew when they'd ever be able to realize that plan? How far down the road would their first child be pushed?

Krissy left for training in Virginia, and about nine months later, returned to Grace Church. If their hopes of having a family were to be fulfilled, it would take a special kind of miracle. How could two young people, just trying to make it, reconcile their demanding careers with their shared desire to become parents? While turning this over in her mind, Krissy recalled the first sermon she had ever heard me preach.

She had never spoken to me before. Like I said, I always felt that Krissy was the reserved type, but that Sunday after returning home, she approached the front for prayer. As I watched her up at the altar, I saw a young lady patiently waiting her turn that reminded me in some ways of my own daughters. She had a deep, pained longing written on her face that I had become pretty familiar with. I approached her.

It was a short conversation, but I'm glad I was prompted to go up to her when I did. Her need was genuine. "I just want to have a family," she kept repeating.

"Are you sure? Because if we do this, I have no doubt that you will have a baby."

She laughed, and I prayed for her. It was that evening that she received a call and the details of her assignment. She would be working Air Force security in South Korea and then go to her subsequent posting in Virginia. The odds seemed to be continually stacking up against her.

Krissy in Korea

Snow gracefully pirouetted in the air as it slowly covered the ground, blanketing the asphalt in a powdery white. The frigid wind tugged at the hood of Krissy's coat, biting at any exposed skin with a stinging intensity. It had been a long day at the Osan Air Base in Pyeongtaek.

She pulled her hood tight against her cheek, clipboard in one hand, flashlight in the other, as a diesel truck rumbled into the checkpoint. With practiced precision, she scanned the undercarriage, checked the cargo seals, and waved the driver through. By the time the taillights disappeared into the snow, her hands were numb.

She had just recently found out that somehow, she would be heading back to the US for a TDY (Temporary Duty). It wasn't anything unusual for someone in her position to be temporarily reassigned, but her orders were certainly a little unprecedented. Instead of being transferred to another base in Korea, she had been assigned to a base in San Antonio. Reassignments like that were rare. Normally, she would've been rotated to another base in Korea, maybe Okinawa at best. It wasn't usual for her to be flown halfway across the world for something like this. And what's more? She would be in the same city her husband was now stationed in. This wasn't standard procedure. This was favor.

She called her husband and found out that he was slated to leave Texas the night she landed. Granted, that took a lot of the magic out of the news for the both of them. *Oh well,* she thought. *At least we'll get to see each other.*

But as it turns out, there was a "backstage operator" on scene with a vested interest in working things out. When Krissy arrived in Texas, she opted for an additional week of leave just to spend more time in the US. At the same time, her husband found himself suddenly without orders. He was commanded to remain at his post until new ones arrived, giving a couple that shouldn't have been able to spend more than a few hours together two whole weeks. A lot can happen in two weeks.

Krissy returned to Korea, pregnant. She spent half of her pregnancy there, serving the country while growing a human. How she managed it, you'll have to ask her yourself. Lord knows, there aren't many who could.

Serving while pregnant brought a new kind of battle. The gear felt heavier, the shifts felt longer, and the biting Korean winter seemed to cut straight through her uniform. Even with the allowances made for her condition, the routine itself was demanding. Long hours on her feet left her back sore and her legs aching. Some mornings, she wrestled with mild nausea, praying quietly for enough strength to get through the shift. Her hand would sometimes involuntarily drift to rest on her stomach, like her body was reminding her of why she needed to push through, who she was really fighting for.

Every day proved to be a challenge, but it wasn't so bad when Krissy had Gabby to count on. As I often say, the answer to almost every prayer is a person (with the ultimate answer to the ultimate problem being Jesus Christ). Without Gabby, Krissy admits that she isn't sure how she would've made it through. The two had been inseparable since boot camp, and during Krissy's pregnancy, Gabby was present at every appointment Krissy had. They did everything together. They ate together, talked constantly, went to church together, etc.

One evening after a routine checkup that the pair had attended together, they sat down in the mess hall to grab a bite. The appointment had gone amazingly, with the doctor reassuring Krissy that all was well with her baby. In the cafeteria, the fluorescent lights hummed overhead, trays clattered, the smell of fried food mixed with the chill of soldiers filing in and out.

"I should be hungry after good news like that." Krissy sighed and pushed a fork through mashed potatoes. "But I guess my stomach just didn't get the memo. I can't even look at this right now."

"Then don't. Just eat the roll. The roll never hurt anybody." Gabby plucked it off of Krissy's tray and ripped it in half, handing a piece back. "I won't lie. That meatloaf might."

Krissy laughed softly, nibbling at the bread.

Gabby took exaggerated bites out of her half of the roll. "Besides, we need you in fighting shape for your trip back home."

"Oh, don't remind me. I still haven't gotten anything back about that. If I don't get on a plane soon, I might be out of time," Krissy said, dropping her head. The rule was clear: After a certain week of pregnancy, flying home wouldn't be allowed. The thought of giving birth overseas, far from Eric and her family, made her chest tighten.

Gabby leaned across the table, lowering her voice so only Krissy could hear. "Hey, stop spiraling."

"I'm not spiraling," Krissy protested halfheartedly.

"You are, Kris. You know it." Gabby smiled knowingly. "You'll get the clearance. You'll get it, and that's a fact. And do you know how?"

Krissy shook her head no.

"The same way you ended up in San Antonio."

Krissy sat silently for a moment. Gabby continued, "You've got someone up there looking out for you. And down here? You've got me."

It's true that God tends to cut it close from time to time, but one evening as the deadline was fast approaching, everything came together. She was cleared, checked out, and on a plane home in two days (a process that normally took weeks for her colleagues) and got home to have her daughter, Alba, on American soil. Krissy was given an honorable discharge, and Gabby ended up taking her spot in Virginia, meaning that she was free to be a mother for the foreseeable future.

How Far We've Come

Krissy's mother lived under the weight of multiple diagnoses such as dissociative identity disorder, schizophrenia, and bipolar disorder. Her father often looked the other way when things went wrong. Growing up in that environment was frightening and unpredictable. She doesn't carry bitterness toward her mother, knowing that much of the pain she caused flowed out of untreated illness rather than malice. Still, the effect was the same: a childhood marked by instability and fear. It is a crushing thing for a child to feel unworthy of protection, to wonder if their needs make them a burden rather than a blessing.

And yet, out of that painful soil grew something redemptive. Krissy has chosen to draw from her past not resentment but compassion. She is intentional with her daughter in small, everyday ways. Krissy listens closely, offers comfort, and affirms Alba's value. She remembers what it felt like to go without those things. Every act of care is her way of saying to Alba, "You are safe. You are wanted. You are loved."

She's been able to find a lot of healing, but it would be a lie to say that all the pain has just disappeared. Even while parenting, she often thinks about the simplest things she longed for as a child—someone to read her a bedtime story, to say, "I'm proud of you," to make her feel safe when the world felt out of control, and for the world to not feel out of control in her own home, where things are meant to make sense. Those moments never came for her, but they became the very things she was determined to give Alba in abundance. The cycle ended with her. Every day, as she watches her daughter grow, she finds herself saying, "I wish I had felt this loved as a kid."

And that in itself is an extended miracle of circumstance. It's about more than making it home in time, the TDY, or paperwork clearing. The true miracle for those of us carrying the cross of nightmare childhoods is the fact that God can take years of brokenness and birth through them the seeds of true love.

Let's not rob God of the credit He deserves for the miracles that go unnoticed. The miracles that fly under the radar. The miracles of circumstance. Krissy often says that her faith has only grown stronger after seeing how favored she felt by God through her whole ordeal. Whenever in doubt that things will work themselves out, she remembers how God was able to "infiltrate the US military" to make things happen for her in the past.

Look What the Lord Has Done

WHEN I BEGAN my pastoral journey about twenty-five years ago, I wasn't hoping to earn myself the unofficial title of "the baby pastor." Looking back, however, I wouldn't have it any other way. It's been a privilege to be a part of stories like the ones you've read here. The fact that God would allow me to be even a small part of His plan in the lives of these beautiful families is truly humbling.

Each story we've covered reveals two fundamental ideas: God's willingness to move in the modern world and the cornerstone status of faith in the Christian walk. And faith? That's something all of us could use just a little more of, whether we're trying to have kids or not. When I offered that first prayer for Debbie Nannery back in 2004, I had no doubt in my mind that God was able and willing to give them their baby. Every prayer I've done since then has been backed by that same level of faith.

But faith isn't the only determining factor in cases like these. The truth is, I've prayed with families who never conceived, and those moments weigh heavy on me. I've seen families go on to find their peace in adoption or a life of service. It's different for different couples. Pastoring means sitting with people in their unanswered prayers just as much as celebrating the ones that are answered. Faith is not pretending we always get the outcome we want, and prayer isn't like making withdrawals from God's ATM. Rather, it is choosing to believe that God's presence has never left us even when the answer is no. Trust means saying, "Not my will, but Yours be done," and resting in the assurance that the One who gave His own Son for us can be trusted with everything else.

And that theme of faith as the ultimate form of relationship with God is explored in different ways in each of these couples' lives. Like a diamond that refracts light differently depending on how you hold it, the wisdom of faith is manifold, multicolored, and multidimensional. It's a gem that has the ability to surprise you in new ways every day.

For some families, faith meant rejecting fear in the face of medical diagnoses. Like in Jesus's miracles of healing and restoration, in their stories, we see that when nature brings finality, God brings new hope. For others, faith meant embracing the fear they felt, negating the hold it had on their minds through secrecy. They took the hidden things and dragged them out into the light, choosing vulnerability and trust. In this, they found true courage. And in other cases, faith took the form of extended waiting and acknowledging God's abilities as a backstage operator who never misses a cue, even when it feels like He has.

These families shocked me with their self-awareness and spiritual insight. Even during the interview process, there were quite a few times that I thought to myself, *Wow, they should be the ones up onstage preaching.* They had drawn out their own lessons from the pressures and battles they'd experienced. As they struggled, they discovered one of the key reasons God allows us to do so. It's rough seas that cause us to cling to the Rock of Ages. It's difficulty that causes us to crave God's presence, and His timely response that shows us His heart—a heart overflowing with love for the brokenhearted and crushed in spirit. A heart that takes joy in family and new life.

We, along with thousands of Christians around the world, have been privileged to experience truly powerful displays of God's ability in very tangible ways. Unlikely childbirth is just scratching the surface! I want you to know that the narrative God is writing through our congregation is far from over. To me, this book is more than just a retelling of specific moments in our collective history, but part of an ongoing story that God isn't done developing.

Waiting

Here's a bit of a pastoral side note about an issue that I find is becoming more and more relevant every year. Something that compounds the issue of pregnancy is the fact that many are waiting way too long to start trying.

> *4 He who observes the wind will not sow, and he who regards the clouds will not reap.*
> **ECCLESIASTES 11:4 (ESV)**

While I agree that there is a time and a place for everything, I'd like to offer a word of caution against waiting for the absolute *perfect* conditions to have a child. Preparation is great, caution is necessary, but those things can start to work against you at some point. You could spend your whole life waiting for the perfect house, minivan, salary, job, etc. You could spend your whole life doing that and run right past the best "parenting years."

I'm not advocating irresponsibility or having kids when you're clearly not prepared to care for another living being. Parents who make that choice often regret it. But I also want to stress that there is no such thing as the "perfect weather." Good farmers know when they have to take initiative and simply sow. If I'd waited till I got every little thing on my checklist done before having kids, I would've run down the biological clock. Let the knowledge that God's got you be an encouragement to take the leap.

Come and See

One of the clearest threads in these stories is that no one walks this journey alone. Every couple was carried by prayer, by community, by friends who stood in the gap. If you are walking a similar road, I want you to know that you don't have to trek it by yourself. Our church family in North Brunswick would be honored to walk with you, to listen, and to pray. Some of our information is included in just a few pages, and whether it's in person or over a phone call, I would love to hear your story and pray with you.

The Son of God

I can't help but think of the story where Jesus healed ten lepers, and only one returned to thank Him. It's human nature to move on quickly once the crisis passes, but I've found that the deepest joy isn't in the miracle itself, but in knowing the Miracle Worker. If these testimonies point you to Jesus, let them also draw you to a lifelong friendship with Him. Gratitude opens the door to relationship, and relationship is where the greatest transformation takes place.

To all that are feeling inspired to seek Jesus and His unparalleled power to transform your life, I just have two requests: Seek Him earnestly, and, if you should find what you seek, be the cleansed leper that came back to give Him thanks. Once you've walked with Jesus long enough, you'll begin to see that miraculous conceptions and miracles of circumstance are just the tip of the iceberg. The transformative power of a life lived with Him is unmatched. For the soul, there's no substitute for that. If it's a miracle that introduces you to the Son of God, let it also be the start of a lifelong journey with Him.

These stories remind me that God is still writing. The same God who gave a child to Abraham and Sarah, to Rebekkah, Rachel, Hannah, and Elizabeth, has not grown weary of giving good gifts.

I pray that you see Him at work in your own story, whether through the miraculous or simply in the quiet. I pray that you experience Him both on the mountains and in the valleys, in successes and in the waiting. I pray that you taste the abundant life with Jesus, and I pray that your home grows to be more and more like a picture of heaven right here on Earth.

In Christ's Name,

Amen

Phone number: +1 (732) 297-9559

Website: www.gracechurchnb.com

Email: info@gracechurchnb.com

About the Authors

JOSEPH CARLUCCI ADEVAI is the Senior Pastor and founder of Grace Church in North Brunswick, New Jersey. A high school dropout turned Wall Street executive, he retired as a Senior Vice President of a Fortune 100 company before answering God's call to ministry. Pastor Joe lives with his wife, Alicia. They have six grown children—Alexandra, Victoria, Jacqueline, Joe, Joshua, and Dominique—and eleven grandchildren.

STEVEN BIJU GEORGE is a writer, musician, and creative leader serving at Grace Church in North Brunswick. Active in church ministry since childhood, he contributes through writing, music, and creative productions. Steven studies business at Rutgers University while also pursuing theological studies. He lives in New Jersey.